# POWER OF INSPIRATION:

## Dare to Be the Best YOU!

D1451013

Various Authors

www.LightPointPress.com

Power of Inspiration: Dare to Be the Best YOU!

Various Authors

Published by Light Point Press
www.LightPointPress.com

Thanks to all who were involved in this project.

Edited by Go Pro Office
www.GoProOffice.com
Thanks Corinne!

Printed in the United States of America

ISBN: 13: 978-0615743226

# Table of Contents

# Introduction

Challenges have been a part of our everyday lives from the very beginning of time. All people will face challenges, from the rich to the poor, from the famous to the anonymous, from the physically fit to the physically challenged. Life can be tough for everyone.

The authors highlighted in this book have all experienced challenges, circumstances and difficulty in their lives and have triumphed in amazing ways. Yet they all have much in common with you. Their days contain 24 hours. They all require food, water and shelter to survive. They have no secret connection to the cosmos. And they are not favored by God more than you.

The turning point for all of these folks was a moment of inspiration in their lives. Whether it was from a teacher who encouraged them to strive for something better or a family member that was there at just the right time – for each there was a defining moment. This moment occurred when each of these people realized that they would no longer be stuck in their circumstances, they would no longer be mired in hopelessness and mediocrity. They would choose to get up, put a stake in the ground and move forward to live a life transformed.

It is the hope of every author in this book that today you would be inspired to live an exceptional life; to live an amazing life, a life that inspires others. If you feel a special connection to anyone in this book, each author has included their contact information at the end of their chapter and would love to connect with you.

It is your choice from this day forward. There are no accidents in life. Everything has a reason. You have this book in your hands at this precise moment in time for a purpose. It is our hope that the Power of Inspiration will cause you to live a life of excellence.

This book is dedicated to Mary Beth who exemplifies the spirit of hope that is within the pages of this book.

# Help Others Get Ahead

By Sandy Anderson

*This chapter is dedicated to countless numbers of Champions who are sitting on the sidelines with a blurry vision because of a great tragedy that came upon their lives. There is hope, healing and purpose waiting in your future.*

My crisis in life started early!

My mother, who was the first school teacher in our little village in India, passed away when I was only one year old. My parents had four sons and my dad did not know what to do with us. When two Indian ladies who ran an orphanage offered to adopt his four children, my dad reluctantly agreed.

A group of Sunday school ladies from America sponsored my way to school, shelter and basic living expenses. I received twelve dollars every month that sustained me. How grateful I am for the precious ladies who had the vision to invest in a child half way across the world and give me a shot at life. I owe them everything for giving me a start.

I grew up better than other children outside the orphanage, but still we were in utter poverty. I didn't have shoes until I was twelve years old. Often we couldn't afford to buy a toothbrush or toothpaste. Sometimes we rubbed two bricks together to clean our teeth; other times we used twigs from trees. Food was limited. We often stole vegetables and fruit from gardens to keep us from the pangs of teenage hunger. We did not eat meat more than a few times a year. Every month we were called to pluck feathers from chickens that were slaughtered by the hundreds. It provided an income toward the self-sustainability of the orphanage. Packaging chicken for commercial purposes was tedious, but we looked forward to those times. We got our taste of meat from disposable sautéed chicken feet cooked on the open fire without any spices. Clean drinking water was scarce. We drank from the well, pond and collected rain water. In the summer, when the water delivery truck came around once a week, we lined up buckets, pitchers or any container available to store water. We gathered water for washing, drinking and bathing, but we also splashed and dumped water on each other causing casual fights and burst of laughter.

We were so poor that we could not afford to buy a soccer ball. Often we made one with cloth, papers and plastic to pad it. When we had a real ball, we played like the famous Pelé of Brazil. Rainy seasons were the most fun. We got soaking wet and raced our "boats" made of leaves and twigs down the drain. At night when the electricity went off, which happened regularly, we played hide and seek. We could not afford to buy real marbles so we played with seeds from the famous banyan trees. The brave among us would catch garden snakes and bottle them up. We had more adventures and fun than modern kids can imagine!

Even in those days, school was boring! Teachers, for the most part, were going through the motions. They would beat us with a stick on our knuckles or head, or even worse throw a wooden duster, chalk or anything close to their fingertips. At times, many of the students would leave the classroom through the windows. Some teachers were so high on drugs that they didn't even notice.

After graduating from school, I got a chance to study in St. Xavier's College in Calcutta – a stone throw distance from Mother Teresa's Missionaries of Charity. I studied commerce and business management. I was an average student in college, but a life changing transformation took place. I had a personal encounter with God and became a follower of Jesus Christ.

Six months later after graduating with a bachelor's degree, I went to visit my brother who was a missionary in the neighboring country of Nepal where Mount Everest is located. It should have only been a short vacation, but when I met the poverty-stricken people, I fell in love with them and was compelled to do something to help them.

Seven days later I relocated myself to Kathmandu, Nepal, to join my two older brothers.

We picked up jobs teaching children in English speaking schools. Immediately, we started a Saturday School (Sunday was a national work day) involving 60-70 children every week. Soon the children were bringing their older siblings to the meetings who were then followed by the adults.

The ministry was growing fast. We did not have any time to teach children at school any more. My brothers and I began to help the people around us. We did not have a lot of resources, but we had a heart to help those in need. We made personal sacrifices and looked for opportunities. In the beginning we could only do a little but God blessed our efforts.

He brought us Ben.

Ben's mother was kicked out of her home when she became a Christian. She did not have any place to go, so she moved in with another relative and brought Ben to our orphan care ministry. At the time, we were sponsoring 50-60 children who had come from difficult backgrounds.

Ben was a frustrated child. He got into trouble easily and fought with other students frequently. The teachers always reported against him and his grades were failing. But at the Love and Hope program, children were called in for devotion every day. Seeds of the Word of God were planted in their young hearts. Ben followed the rest of the children to church as a religious duty but never had a personal conviction about God.

Ben's life was getting worse as he was now into drugs and open rebellion. The school tried everything to change the course of his life but nothing worked. Finally, the breakthrough came when we were hosting a multi-national conference. There were a lot of young people and plenty of good music. Ben was there. When he saw the supernatural miracles of God right in front of his eyes, he too became a follower of Christ.

Ben came to this country with seventy dollars in his pocket. Now he lives with his wife and two boys in Boulder, Colorado. His mother also lives with them. He has thriving restaurants serving Himalayan cuisines. He employs over fifty local college students and hires chefs from Nepal. He supports our ministry sending destitute children to school. Benjamin has come full circle.

This is what is so great about helping others. When we extend a small gesture of love and compassion to others, we can help them reach their destiny. I have found helping others is one of life's most awesome privileges.

Many well-meaning people wait for an opportune time to respond to someone in need. They think, *when my kids are older, when my business becomes more productive, when I retire, I will give back to society.* The danger in this type of mindset is when you overcome one challenge, another one will arise. The best time to help someone is now. Yesterday is gone, tomorrow is not guaranteed – "now" is all you are in control of. If you plant a seed now, one day you will reap a harvest.

Andrew Valdez was born in New Mexico but moved to Salt Lake City, Utah. Losing his father at a young age forced Andrew to work on the street as a shoe-shiner. At the age of eight, he began selling newspapers in Salt Lake City. One day when Valdez was ten years old, he met a man named Jack Keller. Jack was always dressed in a suit and had a newspaper in his hand. One day the boy asked him, "Hey Mister, why don't you buy a paper from me?" Wanting to help the street kid, Jack became his regular customer. As the relationship developed, Keller took Valdez under his wing and introduced him to the world of tennis and folks at the country club. Valdez excelled in tennis, but he could not help but notice that the best dressed people at the country club were lawyers. So he decided to become a lawyer. Consequently with the help of Keller's mentoring, Valdez entered Law School at the University of Utah and went on to become a successful lawyer.

Over the years they lost track of each other. Forty years later, everything came full circle when Andy, found Jack Keller begging in front of a store. He was filthy and suffering from dementia. Immediately, Andy took Jack off the streets and provided Jack care and dignity for the remainder of his life. Today, Judge Andrew Valdez deals with troubled kids, giving help and being a role model for them to become contributing members in society. Judge Valdez's story reminds us that with the help and love of another, anyone can achieve anything in life. It is also a reminder to each of us of where we came from and who helped us along the way. No matter who we are, what color our skin or what our country of origin is, there are far more similarities than differences between us.

I have found God will bring people into our lives that are directly linked to our own destiny. These people are not necessarily to help us but for us to help them. Our progress lies in their success. We may have to open some doors for them. It means, we have to introducing them to someone we know. The more efficiently and willingly we help them, the faster and higher we are going to go. Pushing them up will automatically take us to a higher level. Over the course of my life, I've had hundreds of people pushing me up. In return, I've dedicated my life to serve those who have no voice and little opportunities.

You may say, *"Sandy, when will someone help me? I have no one to help me!"* But you do. None of us got here on our own. Someone made a positive deposit in your life. Had it not been for that person, you wouldn't be here today. Best of all, the Creator of the universe, God Almighty is not only with you, but He also is *for* you. Jesus said, *"I will never leave you nor forsake you."* (Hebrews 13:5).

At times we are wrong to think that we do not have enough in ourselves to help someone else. This may sound logical, but it underestimates the power in you. I have found that life is a combination of tiny miracles. What we do for others, God will cause others do for us.

Prasad came from a destitute family in India. He could not finish school for lack of opportunity. I met him in the early nineties when he was working as a driver for a friend. I was impressed by his commitment to serve and learn. Officially he was a driver, but you could count on him for anything. He was always willing and ready to work hard.

One day I introduced him to one of my friends from Oregon, who was visiting Nepal. Their friendship developed and my friend offered him a chance to come to America. Prasad was very excited but he had many setbacks. For starters, he could not speak English, much less read or write. He asked me to help him fill out his visa application form. Miraculously, Prasad got a visa to come to America.

After nine months and less than a hundred dollars to his name, Prasad moved to New York to be with Dave, another friend he had met through our ministry. One day Dave took him to a construction site where his father was pouring concrete. Immediately Prasad jumped in to help. Dave's father was so impressed with Prasad that he offered him a job on the spot.

Fast forward a few years, Prasad learned English, passed the GED test and even enrolled himself in a community college. Several years later, he was running his own construction company worth millions of dollars. Today, he is giving hope to the less fortunate through our ministry. Prasad has come full circle.

Think about it! It did not take a lot of time on my part, but simply by caring for someone in need the door opened for him to come to America. When we help others, we ignite a chain of miracles that touch and inspire many. You may not have a million dollars to give to your favorite charity right now, but can you help someone fill out their application form? Do not talk yourself out of offering your help because sometimes it is our small acts of kindness that bring out the greatness in people.

Once, the Israelites were fighting a battle with the Amalekites. Moses, the leader, had a deal with God. As long as Moses held his rod and arms up in the air, the Israelites prevailed. But when his arms came down, the enemy had the advantage. Assessing the situation, Aaron, Moses' brother, and Hur came to help. When he tired, they held up the heavy arms of Moses. Amazingly, this small act of service brought about a great victory for the whole nation of Israel. (Exodus 15:8-13).

I wonder how the battle would have ended if Aaron and Hur thought, *Man, I have no education. I come from a dysfunctional family. I have no war experience. I do not even know how to shoot an arrow. I have nothing to offer in this tensed situation.* No. Instead, they had a serving attitude. They simply offered what they could and God made it to be a battle winning strategy. This is what happens when we reach out to others with what God has given us.

When I was in grade school; boys and girls alike had to learn sewing. Being a boy, it did not come easy for me. But I had an extra-ordinary teacher named Ms. Grape. In every sewing class, she stood by me and helped me finish my sewing project. She told me I could do it and showed me how. She invested extra time on me teaching me to sew. Years later, I not only learnt how to sew; but I remember Ms. Grape's kindness. I couldn't repay her then but now she is honored by your reading about her.

Friend, look for ways to be good to people. You may not be able to give a job to someone, but like Jack Keller, can you buy "newspaper" from somebody who needs that income. You may not be able to fight a war, but like Aaron and Hur, you can lift someone up who is going through a battle in life. You may not be able to send someone to college, but like my teacher Ms. Grape, you can teach someone, something practical that you know.

Sometimes, in order to help people, you have to get out of your comfort zone. Those who are in need may not come knocking on the front door of your house, but God will put people on your path throughout the day where you can let your kindness shine.

My friend Martha has a heart of gold. She has a wonderful family and always jumps at any opportunity to help others. She and her husband have a dental practice. Recently, she told me how she had stopped by at a fast food restaurant on her way to pick up her kids from school. As she was waiting to order her food, she noticed a huge, tall man, clothing in disarray, sitting at a table struggling to fill out a job application.

Martha is a petite young lady, but she was drawn to help this stranger. I'm sure she felt a little intimidated but she pushed through her inhibition. As she helped the stranger fill out a job application, she learned that he had been a truck driver. He had recently lost his license. He was applying for a job at the fast food restaurant because he needed $350 to get his driving license back.

Martha has a strange habit. Every once in a while, when she comes across a hundred dollar bill, she hides it in her purse hoping that one day she would treat herself to something nice – a pedicure, lunch with a friend or a special dress she had spotted on sale. When Martha started helping this stranger, she felt God was speaking to her in a small voice. *Give the hundred dollars in your purse to help this man.* Her first thought was, *Get behind me Satan!* It was out of her comfort zone. She opened her purse reaching for the hundred dollars she had hidden. Miraculously, she found not one, but three one hundred dollar bills. Now she was certain that Satan himself was speaking to her mind, but Martha is such a natural giver that she did not entertain that thought for more than a second, she helped the stranger fill out his job application and handed him three hundred dollars cash! She did not know the end of this story, but I know for certain that Martha had paid it forward. One day when she or her children will need it the most, God will make sure to care for her and her family. Next time you pass by an eighteen wheeler truck be gentle and show a little kindness. It could be Martha's truck driver whom she put back on the road.

I tell you my friend; this is what made America so great – neighbor helping neighbor. We care about each other even if we are total strangers. We reach out. We help, give generously, sacrificially and willingly. When we live life intentionally like Martha, God Himself will make it His personal project to help us in our time of need.

You don't necessarily have to do anything big – buy someone a lunch. Give a ride to someone; take them to church. Bake a cake for your elderly neighbor. If you meet a stranger, introduce them to someone you know who can help them. Like Jack Keller, mentor someone. Speak well of somebody when others are speaking down on that person. Friend, when you're good to people, you'll store up rewards for yourself. One day those rewards, gathering up in clouds, will get so thick and heavy that it will begin to rain down on your life. It will refresh you when you are going through your worst. God wants to be good to you; but first, you must plant a few seeds. The scripture says, *"You will always harvest what you plant."*

I have learned that sometimes some of our experiences can become a stumbling block in helping others. We all know people who have taken advantage of us. They have taken our generosity for granted. Others have lacked integrity and manipulated us unfairly. We all have met such individuals. Learn from them. Do not be naive. But do not allow them to harden you. Cultivate a tender heart. When we shut our hearts of compassion, we isolate and hurt ourselves in the long run.

In the scriptures, there is a beautiful story of friendship and loyalty. When you sow into other people's lives it will bless your family members for generations to come.

In this story, a shepherd boy named David is chosen by Prophet Samuel to be the next king of Israel. David goes to a hero's status overnight when he kills giant Goliath. Saul, the reigning king, starts to feel insecure and makes multiple attempts to take David's life. Let me pause here for a moment and let you in on a secret. When God begins to show His favor and prosper you, all kinds of haters and enemies will come out of the woodworks. When you feel that others are pulling you down, remind yourself saying, *the only time people can pull me down is when I am ahead of them!* Do not respond to your critics who are not for you.

In the duration of multiple assassination plots, Jonathan, King Saul's son, becomes David's closest ally. He keeps David a step ahead by informing him of his father's secret plots to kill him. One day in a fierce battle both Saul and his son, Jonathan, are killed and David is crowned as the next king of Israel.

Fast forward a few years. David is firmly established on the throne as the king of Israel. He is not hiding in caves, or running from Saul who is bent on taking his life. At the palace he has more time to reminisce on his life and what brought him there. He reflects on his closest friend, brother and ally, Jonathan. He chokes up at the memory of him and the friendship they shared. Finally, David is so full of gratitude toward his friend Jonathan; he asks his cabinet, *"Is there still anyone who is left of the house of Saul, that I may show him kindness for Jonathan's sake"* (2 Samuel 9:1-13 NKJV)?

Sure enough they track down Jonathan's ancestral home and learn that one of his sons Mephibosheth is still alive but crippled in his feet. When he arrives at the palace, Mephibosheth is terrified for his life and throws himself in front of David. He is thinking, *certainly David is going to execute me after all that my grandfather did to harm his life.* Instead, he is welcomed and assured by David that no harm will come to him or any of his family members. David extends his loyalty and mercy for the sake of his best friend Jonathan. Mephibosheth moves in to the palace and eats at the king's table. David also restores the land to Mephibosheth that belonged to his fathers.

Friend, do not pay people back for their crimes. Instead, show mercy. Like King David, plant a seed of kindness even when your friends do not deserve it. No matter how imperfect your family and friends may be, without them, you will not be where you are today. When you have climbed the mountain of your success, reach out and help someone else get to the top. Be a loyal friend to somebody. You may not see the results right away, but I can assure you that like Jonathan, your children and your children's children will benefit from your loyalty.

One of the greatest gifts you can give to people is your listening ears and encouragement. People get beat down at home, work and at play. In the stress-filled world that we live in today, it is very easy for people to feel down, discouraged and defeated. You can create an instant miracle when you take the time to listen to a stressed out friend or let them vent. Just being there and listening to their frustration without being judgmental or offering a solution is divine.

Recently I was visiting a friend in Germany. We have known each other for over twenty years. My friend is a minister like me. He has accomplished unbelievable success in his ministry. But he is a loner. He does not have many close friends. While I was visiting him, we touched on a sore subject and he got really upset. He shook his fingers at me and shouted me down. I knew my dear friend was under stress. I put on a brave front and let him vent for a while. In fact, I encouraged him to get it all out of his chest. He had pent up frustration for years. He did not feel safe to let off steam with anybody. I was glad that he felt comfortable to vent with me.

Immediately afterwards, he calmed down. We talked like best friends. We discussed many deep issues concerning his life. By the time I left, he couldn't thank me enough for my friendship and listening ears. He was able to pin point four or five major issues that were causing stress in his life. I left feeling better knowing that I was able to invest into my friend's life.

Everyone wants to be on the receiving end of the Golden Rule, but it is of little effect until you learn to be on the giving end. When I minister, often people ask me, "When will it happen to me? When do you think others will help me?" The famous Zig Zigler said, "You will always have what you want if you help others get what they want." If you want to live a satisfied life, use your influence to help others achieve their success.

Be a little more giving than you have to be.

Get up each day asking, "Lord, who can I be a blessing to today? Show me how I can help someone." I can assure you, there will be someone in the slow traffic you can let squeeze in front of you. At your work make an extra coffee for your co-worker. Buy someone lunch. You say, *"These people are mean. They've done me wrong."* Do it anyways; your giving will rub off on them. God will begin to mend relationship, and you will gather more than you scatter.

The Scripture says in John 3:16, *"For God so loved the world that He gave..."* You, too, are most like God when you give back. Give generously. Give sacrificially and give secretly. There is a special reward awaiting you when you give without getting credit for it. God sees what you do in secret, and He will reward you openly.

In his book *"I'm No Hero"* U.S. Navy jet pilot Captain Charles Plumb tells the story of his flaming plane going down in the enemy territory of Vietnam War zone. After seventy five combat missions, in the dense jungles of Vietnam, he was shot down by a surface-to-air missile. Plumb ejected and parachuted himself out of the flaming jet only to glide himself in the enemy's camp. He was captured as a POW. He was tortured beyond humane, but somehow he survived the horrific six years in a communist Vietnamese prison.

One day Plumb and his wife were enjoying a meal together in a restaurant. A young man from another table walked up to theirs and said, "You're Plumb. You are a fighter jet pilot. You carried out missions in Vietnam from the aircraft carrier Kitty Hawk. Your jet was shot down!"

Perplexed, Plum asked, "Who are you? How did you know all this?"

The young man replied, "I packed your parachute sir. I guess it worked!"

Filled with gratitude Plumb replied, "Yes it did! If your chute hadn't worked, I wouldn't be here today."

The rest of the day Plumb walked around in daze. That night he could not sleep, thinking about the young sailor who saved his life. How many times Plumb walked passed those sailors in navy uniform with a bib flipped backward and didn't even bother to say, "Good morning, how are you?" or shake their hand? In his mind, he was a fighter jet pilot – a class apart from the lowly sailors. He began to imagine how the sailors who spent long hours delicately weaving the material and packing the silks of each chute. At the end of the tireless and monotonous completion, the sailor who held the life itself of someone whom he did not even know.

Today Plumb lectures to thousands crisscrossing the country asking this one question: "Who is packing your parachute?" Sometimes in the daily challenges of life, we miss what is really important. We fail to say hello, please, or thank you, congratulate someone on something wonderful that has happened to them, give a compliment, or just do something kind for no reason. Don't let that be you.

You see, in life we all have people behind us who packs our physical, mental, emotional and spiritual parachute. None of us made it here on our own. When you look back at the long line of people who have helped you this far, it is only fitting to think how you can help someone else. Your life today is the aggregate of God's goodness and the kindness, sacrifices and investment of scores of people. Some of the first people we forget or neglect the most are our immediate family. Yet, they sacrifice the most in our success. Let us recognize value and compliment members of our family every day. It is not enough to be grateful to them in our hearts; we must express to them what they mean to us.  But don't stop there. It is time now to reach out and help a friend and even the less fortunate on the other side of the globe.  It is time to help others get ahead.

Let me leave you with a quote from a must read book, *City of Joy* depicting the extra-ordinary celebration of slum life in Calcutta, India.

*All that is not given is lost! ~ Hasari Pal*

Sandy Anderson is the Founder/President of Build International Ministries. He is a writer, sought after speaker, and minister. He has ministered in over 40 countries in the world. Sandy's life aspiration is to empower others to become all that God created them to be. His Life Lessons Radio broadcast reaches millions in Asia every week.

We invite you to become a vision partner with Build International Ministries. You can transform a community by providing clean drinking water, education, creating jobs, preventive medical care, spiritual development and much more. You will be amazed how in a small way of involvement you can make an eternal impact.

**Sandy Anderson, Founder & President**
Build International Ministries
972-800-4346
Email: buildinternational@sbcglobal.net
Website: www.buildinternational.org

Follow Sandy:
www.facebook.com/pages/BUILD-International-
Ministries/113937368637778
Twitter: @buildintl

# "Lo and Behold"

By Jeanette Bailey

*This is dedicated to all of you who may feel discouraged by the circumstances of your lives, to those who are still searching for your higher calling and purpose, to those who have been patiently waiting on the Lord to open a door for you to do what you feel He is calling you to do, and to all those who have taken a 'leap of faith' and started on the very rewarding, but somewhat lonely, journey of doing something completely unique and different! God bless you all, and may you find peace, contentment, and joy in the journey!!*

I love that old hymn "Standing on the Promises." It's always a good reminder to me that the Bible is full of so many wonderful promises and that the promises are true! God is good. He is faithful. He will never leave you or forsake you. He has a plan and a purpose for your life. You have a great future in store and He will guide you step by step, but He may choose to only shine the light directly on the step where you are placing your foot at that moment. I also love the old expression "Lo and Behold." You read about it in the passage when the angel came to Mary and told her she was going to bear a son saying "and behold, thou shalt conceive in thy womb, and bring forth a son, and shalt call his name Jesus" (Luke 1:31) and also in the following verse "and behold, thy cousin Elizabeth, she hath also conceived a son in her old age" (Luke 1: 36). You read it again when the angel proclaimed Jesus' birth to the shepherds "And, lo, the angel of the Lord came upon them, and the glory of the Lord shone around them" (Luke

2:9). Now I'm not saying that I've witnessed anything as earth-shattering or world-changing as the birth of the Son of God. I'm just telling you what God has done in my life. The Bible tells us the many miraculous things God has done in the lives of His people. Even today, our lives are testimonies that He continues to work in and through us and that miracles happen every day! There are so many things to say and stories I could tell, but this is just the condensed *Reader's Digest* version of some of the things He has done in my life.

## HE PREPARES

### Nursing Career

I suffered the loss of my first child, my daughter, when she was 2 ½ years old. She was born with a congenital heart defect, and after caring for her night and day through her 30 months of life, this was the most significant and heartbreaking loss I had ever experienced. I was devastated. At one point, I was so distraught that I even contemplated suicide. But somehow, by the grace of God, I survived that horribly tragic time in my life. Our family also suffered through some other serious and often very miserable circumstances during the next ten years. I'm happy to report that, despite the many hardships, difficult times, and "close calls," we all survived and were lifted up out of the pit of darkness we were in. I'm also happy to report that one year after my daughter passed away, I delivered my son, a healthy baby boy, and he has been one of the greatest joys and blessings of my life! When he turned one year old, I started nursing school, graduated with highest honors, and then spent the next 16 years of my career working as an RN.

After graduation, I worked in the hospital setting on the Pediatric Medical/Surgical floor, and then in Pediatric ICU. Because of my experiences with the chronic illness of my daughter, being in and out of the hospital numerous times and then losing her, I could truly empathize with the parents and families. I knew first-hand what they were experiencing with their children going through critical, life-threatening illnesses.

When I moved to a small town where there were no pediatric hospitals nearby, several ladies at my church recommended I apply at a local hospice agency. I went to work as a hospice nurse and for the next 5 years I cared for many patients and their families. Most of the patients were elderly, so I transitioned from working exclusively with children who were receiving aggressive, life-saving treatments, to the senior adults who were at the end of their lives and needed palliative care and comfort measures, with a strong emphasis on spiritual and emotional care of the whole family.

Following the 5 years of hospice nursing, I worked home health and then went back to the hospital setting and worked on the adult medical/surgical floor and then adult ICU. When I relocated to the DFW Metroplex, I was offered a position as an elementary school nurse and I spent the next 7 years caring for children ranging in ages from 4 to 12 years old.

## **Music Career**

From an early age, I have always loved music. I guess you could say I had somewhat of a musical family. My mom played piano at our church and my dad loved singing. I have fond memories of listening to mom playing piano in our living room; she played so beautifully. I took lessons for a couple of years in elementary school, hoping that someday I could play like my mom, but I'm still not even close. My dad used to serenade us kids on a regular basis. Sometimes he sang silly songs like *Do Your Ears Hang Low?*, sometimes popular theme songs from TV shows like *Raw Hide* and movies like *Oklahoma* singing *O What A Beautiful Morning* at the top of his lungs when my sister and I wouldn't get out of bed. Sometimes he did impersonations of Elvis like *You Ain't Nothing But a Hound Dog* or Jerry Lee Lewis' *Great Balls of Fire*! I remember as a young child listening to records for hours at a time both at home and at my grandmother's house. I also watched musical TV shows like *Lawrence Welk* and all kinds of movie musicals, like *The Wizard of Oz* and *The Sound of Music*. I remember snuggling up close to the record player and the radio and memorizing whole movie sound tracks, entire record albums, and hundreds of songs. My sister would also teach me all of the silly songs she learned at Girl Scout camp and I added those to my repertoire!

When I started school, music class was one of my favorite subjects. Our music teacher had us learn all kinds of songs from different countries, some with 10 or 15 verses, and I would memorize each one and then serenade my family, my friends, my pigs, my cows, my cat, just anyone who would listen (or pretend to listen). When I was in 4th grade, my mom recruited me for both the youth and the adult church choirs, where I started learning to sing the alto part and harmonize with the melody. I just seemed to have a knack for music and I loved it so much!

When I was in junior high I signed up for band and asked to play the drums. And for the next 3 years I think I about drove my family crazy beating on everything in our house to practice, practice, practice all the rhythm patterns our band director assigned. When I was a senior in high school, I joined the choir, and there I received my first official voice training and even took a few private lessons at a local community college. I also joined a little music band and we sang at a few local gigs.

As an adult, I always sang in the choirs of the various small churches I attended. I eventually began directing the children's choirs and then was asked to direct the adult and children's hand bell choirs, and added first an adult choir and then another. In addition, I was offered a position as General Music teacher and Chapel director at a small, local private Christian school and I served there for a year, before going back to my nursing career. I also started taking some piano and voice lessons at the local community college just to practice and hone my skills, and for a short time I sang with a large community choir.

## Flowers & Decorating

My grandmother always had flowers in her garden, and I remember going out onto her patio and watching her tend her flower beds and potted plants. I grew up in the country and we had a big vegetable garden, but also a few rose bushes and crepe myrtles, and I remember how much I liked the flowers and watching things grow. I can also remember sitting at our kitchen table and smelling up the whole house as I painted with oils onto small canvases, then displaying my "works of art" around the house. Art was another one of my favorite interests in elementary school, and I also took art class as an elective in both junior high and high school. Later as an adult, I began to make lots of things by hand and enjoyed making many types of crafts, from stained glass to wooden nativity sets to needle work and sewing. I even trained to be a jeweler and for a time I worked at the small jewelry store that my parents owned. I just seemed to have a knack for making things by hand and making things look pretty. My mom always told me, "You should be a decorator or own a flower shop!"

## Mission trips to Japan

While working as a school nurse, I had the opportunity to minister on mission trips during the summers. My son had developed a strong interest in Japan and learning Japanese. Miraculously, the Lord put just the right people in our path at just the right time. Amazing things happened like a Speech Therapist at our school who had gone on many short term mission trips told me about the organization she went with, and it turned out the founders were members of my church. Then one day while standing in the church parking lot talking to a friend who had also mentioned the same organization and the same couple who founded it, "Lo and Behold" if they didn't walk up to us at just that very moment and introduce themselves and tell me how to get connected with their organization. (Mind you, we were in a parking lot full of hundreds of cars and on the complete opposite side of the building where I normally park. This was a divine connection!)

My 16 year old son and I went on our first mission trip together that summer (along with the Speech Therapist I told you about previously.) We asked to go to Japan and that's where they sent us! We went every summer for the next 5 years, sometimes on the same team, sometimes not. The goal of the mission trips was to introduce others to Christ by sharing the stories of Jesus in the Bible and also to build friendships with the people and share our own personal experiences of how God has worked in our lives, His amazing love and grace, and the hope we have for the future. I loved getting to know my new Japanese friends, building relationships with them, reading the Bible together, encouraging them, and praying with them and for them. Each year, I just wanted to stay there and continue the work we had begun and build the relationships we had started. It was such a wonderfully rewarding experience, and I just seemed to have a knack for it. I was even told by one of the pastors of our host church, "You would be a good one to come and do this full time."

Initially, my husband was not very receptive to the idea of me going to a foreign country to do mission work. But, by the second summer, while my son was preparing to join a team, my husband had a change of heart and encouraged me to go, as well. He even gave me a laptop computer and signed us up for *Skype* so that we could talk to each other on the computer. By the fourth year, he agreed to have me stay for an entire 6-weeks project, and even asked if he could come over and visit me! So, he came to Japan to visit me that summer, and within about 10 minutes after getting off the bus from the airport, he said, "Honey, I love this place! I think we should move here!" Oh, my goodness! I was so excited! Not only was my husband supportive of me going on the mission trips, but now he was stating emphatically that we should move over there! Little did he know that each summer I just wanted to stay in Japan and that I had been praying to move there ever since that first trip. The Lord totally changed his heart and mind about this, and all without me ever saying a word to him about it! It is so amazing how God works in the lives of His people!

## My Search

So we started taking Japanese language classes and actively seeking gainful employment in Japan. It was a 1-year roller coaster ride for us, with getting our hopes up and then be disappointed when the potential job opportunities didn't pan out. After numerous attempts, and making many contacts, I found an "English teacher" position. However, the salary that was offered was not enough for two people to live on in the Japanese economy. In addition, even though the company where my husband worked had operations in Japan, he was turned down over and over again for a work Visa. We were really starting to get discouraged. Having resigned from my full time nursing position with the local school district thinking I was moving to Japan, we were really starting to feel the pressure of uncertainty and being in limbo. Many months later, in March 2011, when the earthquake and tsunami hit Japan and devastated a large section of the main island, I finally understood why God had not opened a door for us at that particular time. He was protecting us and also preparing us for something in the future.

## HE CALLS

My earnest prayer had been that God would open a door for us in Japan, because I really felt that was where He was calling me to serve. When my husband came on board with the idea, I thought that was the confirmation I had been looking for. However, the door did not open, and in fact the door was closed over and over again. I remember praying "Lord, I thought you were calling me to Japan. I've quit my full time job, and I'm obviously not in Japan. What am I supposed to be doing?"

Then "Lo and Behold," one sleepless night 2 years ago (August 2010 to be exact) just after I had received my last paycheck from the school district, I received an idea that I knew was from the Lord, because it wasn't something I would have ever thought of myself. I was wide awake; I didn't hear voices nor did I see a vision. But the idea came into my mind suddenly and with great clarity and detail, including what I would be doing and even the name, "Angel Wing." I would be making and delivering flower arrangements to people who are sick, hurting, lonely, grieving, or just needing some encouragement and a little extra TLC. I would visit with them and let them know that someone cares, that they are remembered, and that God loves them. I knew I would also sing hymns, read scriptures, and have a prayer time with the people I visit. It was a perfect combination of all the things I love doing and that God had been preparing me to do my whole life! He was combining my love of music, making things by hand that look pretty, and sharing God's love through scripture, prayer, and words of hope and encouragement. Not only that, he was using my experiences I had with my daughter and all those years I spent working as a nurse. He had been preparing me so that I could now go into hospitals, nursing homes, hospice units, Alzheimer's units, and private homes in order to minister to the spiritual and emotional needs of clients and their families. Places where others may feel overwhelmed or intimidated were very familiar to me. I would be visiting people of all ages (from newborns to centurions,) in all settings (from ICU to private homes,) and in all stages of life (from the crib beside mother's bed to the bedside of someone taking their last breaths.) Wow!!! This idea He gave me was so exciting that I frantically began writing notes so that I wouldn't forget any of the details.

I spent the next three days thinking and praying about this new idea. Thoughts, doubts, and questions kept running through my mind: "After all, Lord, I'm not a trained business woman, a licensed florist, a professional musician, or an ordained minister." I kept thinking, "Lord, am I qualified or talented enough to start such a venture??" Another BIG question was: "how is my husband going to respond?" Being the pragmatic, analytical type, he can ask lots of hard questions and can think of a hundred reasons why something won't work or why it's not feasible or logical, and to me that seems very discouraging. I actually anticipated that he would be a nay-sayer and think of all the reasons why I shouldn't pursue it. Plus, he really doesn't like surprises, so I thought it would not go over well with him.

When I finally decided it was time to reveal the idea to my husband, I had my notes in hand, and asked him to sit down. I told him I needed to talk to him about something important, and I asked him to please not interrupt and to let me finish my little presentation before he started asking questions. Several times he asked, "what about this?" and "what about that?" and "how's it going to work?" But after my little *spiel* was over, he just sat there and stared at me in silence for what seemed like a very long time. (It was probably only a couple of minutes, but it seemed like forever). I was really nervous and wondered how he was going to respond. Much to my surprise, he looked right at me and said, "Honey, I think it's a great idea. I think you should go for it!" Oh, my goodness! I was in shock!! I was so happy and excited, and I knew that this was definitely confirmation from the Lord, because it's very uncharacteristic of my husband to quickly accept an idea that is totally unexpected and out of the blue!!

## HE EQUIPS

I'm sure you have heard this famous old saying many times: "The Lord doesn't necessarily call those who are qualified, but He qualifies those He calls." He has shown me over and over again that I don't have to have all the answers, because I know the One who does. I can trust that He will send the Holy Spirit to guide me and show me the way. He has a purpose and a plan for my life, and all I need do is to be obedient to the call, and to use the ideas, the desires, and the gifts and talents He has placed in my body, my mind, and my heart for His glory. He then sends the people to help at just the right time and in such amazing and surprising ways!

As I said, I didn't feel particularly qualified to start my own company. In fact, I was relatively clueless about strategic planning, networking, marketing, social media, accounting, or any of the things required to run a small business. Never-the-less, I immediately began taking the preliminary steps in preparing to launch "Angel Wing Florals, Visits, & Psalms." I opened a bank account, hooked up a phone line, applied for my d.b.a. and State tax exempt status, purchased a liability insurance policy, designed a logo, had my son start working on a website, and had some business cards and brochures printed. I officially began as a for-profit business in January 2011, and started joining community networking groups, selling flower arrangements, and taking appointments to go and visit people in hospitals, nursing homes, private homes, Alzheimer's units, and Hospices. However, there was something deep inside that I just didn't feel right about. Over the course of several months, there were some specific signs that let me know that God was calling me to do this as a *ministry* and not a for-profit *business*.

After showing me that this really is a ministry and should be a not-for-profit organization, "Lo and Behold" God suddenly brought into my path a lady that I had not seen nor had any contact with in 32 years!! She and I went to junior high and high school together. Miraculously and unbeknownst to me, she was to be the guest speaker at a women's networking group that I had regularly attended for several months. I recognized her right away, and struck up a conversation, and we reminisced about our school days and classmates, etc. She told me that several years ago she had started a ministry that is a resource for women who want to have their own ministries, and that she helps them get started and allows them to come under the organization's non-profit 501(c)(3) umbrella. I felt this was a divine connection! This was my confirmation of what God had been revealing to me over the past few months, and so I applied for membership and was approved by their board of directors. Angel Wing became an alliance partner with this group. The icing on the cake was when I was driving over to sign the agreement to become an alliance partner, I looked up in the sky and there was a huge cloud that was shaped like a giant hand hovering over the place where I was going. The funny thing was, there were no other clouds in the sky! I remember crying and saying over and over "The hand of God is over me....the hand of God is over me." I wished I would have taken a picture of it! That was in August 2011, which was exactly one year after God first gave me the idea for Angel Wing.

Since operating as a 501(c)(3) non-profit organization, the Lord has continued to show His favor and showered us with many blessings. He has been so faithful to provide everything we have needed, including a new position for my husband that saved him from the sweeping layoffs that his company underwent following the announcement that they were filing bankruptcy. We were so surprised when one day, out of the blue, he received a phone call and was asked to interview for a job that he didn't even know existed. He went for the interview and a few days later they offered him the job AND a raise AND a change of location! All this occurred a few weeks before the company made the official announcement that they were filing for bankruptcy, started laying off hundreds of employees, and announced they were closing the facility where my husband had worked for the past 20 years. Looking back on it, we realized that God was working on our behalf and orchestrating behind the scenes in ways that we were totally unaware of at that time. Though the company remains in turmoil and the outcome uncertain, we continue to rejoice and celebrate because my husband just recently celebrated his 25th anniversary with the company, which is a major career milestone!

God is so good and so faithful. He sustained and provided for us after I quit my nursing job. He even honored us with a new position for my husband and an increase in his salary which allowed us to have enough income to pay our monthly bills. Also, when my husband was having problems with his vision and needed to have surgery to remove a cataract, we weren't sure where the money would come from. But "Lo and Behold," the lady who helped us file our tax return found a mistake on the previous year's return, and we received a refund in the amount of what we owed for the eye surgery!

Meanwhile, the Lord has been opening doors and providing for Angel Wing ministry in wonderful and amazing ways. He has brought the funds needed to sustain the organization and sometimes this happens in such surprising and unexpected ways (such as donated items from a very popular country music band which we used to raise money, but that is another totally amazing story.) Local business owners (one in particular who gave donations two weeks in a row) and other individuals in the community have made financial contributions and participated in our fundraising events. God also put in my path the strong Christian business people who came alongside me, encouraged me, and served on my first advisory board. I also met a leadership executive coach who offered his services pro-bono in order to help with developing a 5-year strategic plan for Angel Wing. This gentleman, who is now a member of my governing board, helped me focus in on and write the vision and mission statements that God had placed in my heart, as well as the goals and action steps necessary to bring them to fruition. Through that process, the Lord has shown me that someday there will be an "army of angels" going out and bringing comfort, compassion, hope, and encouragement to those in need. He is opening doors and providing avenues to bless people of all ages, including people who live in facilities away from their homes and families, children who have been abused, college students who are looking for volunteer opportunities and people who just want to make a difference in the lives of others.

As I said, there are so many more amazing stories I could tell you. The stories are testimonies of God's goodness, mercy, and faithfulness, such as the time last April when a group of volunteers gathered at a local church to assemble Easter baskets for abused and underprivileged kids. We were in an area that was hit by approximately 17 tornadoes that day. Yet, miraculously, the building we were in sustained no damage, and even though we had to seek shelter in the women's restroom while the alarm sirens were sounding, the terrible storms passed and we were still able to finish the baskets and deliver them all on time!!

God continues to remind me over and over that this is a true calling and that it touches lives in such a deep and meaningful way. It's so heartwarming to hear people express their gratitude and appreciation and say things like: "My grandmother called me four times to thank me for sending you to visit her at the retirement home;" the sweet little lady who said, "I've been kind of depressed lately, but I know God answered my prayers because you came to visit me today;" and the precious woman who said, "I've been in the hospital for a while now but this is the best medicine I've had!" It seems to really mean a lot to people when I ask if I can add them to our prayer list and have our prayer team continue to pray for them. The wonderful answers to prayer are such a testimony of God's healing and grace, such as the young lady who had been in the hospital for over a month waiting for a liver transplant. Towards the end of my visit with her she said "When I was a little girl I used to love going to church with my aunt, but I haven't gone in years and years. Hearing the hymns, reading the scriptures, and having you pray with me brings back fond memories.

I'm not sure if I'm a Christian, but if I ever get to go home from the hospital, I want to start taking my boys to church." I continued to keep her in my prayers, and I found out that a few weeks after my visit she became very ill and almost died. But "Lo and Behold" they found a donor just in the nick of time and guess what? ... many months later I found out that she was baptized!

Throughout this journey, God has given me the desires of my heart and also a much larger vision for the expansion of Angel Wing to our surrounding communities, other cities, and eventually to Japan! While working through the process of developing a strategic plan, I realized that one of the next steps would be to apply for my own 501(c)(3) status. Then "Lo and Behold" God put in my path a young man I had not seen in years. His parents go to my church and they're the founders of the organization I told you about that provided the opportunities for us to do mission trips to Japan! There he was at an early morning networking meeting, and I recognized him and we struck up a conversation. When I asked him why he was at the meeting, he told me that he has a company and helps people start their own 501(c)(3) organizations. Another divine connection! It's so amazing how the Lord puts people in your path at just the right time.

So with the help of this young man, I started the application process. (This was just one year after becoming an alliance partner of the larger 501(c)(3) organization I mentioned previously.) When the first part of the paperwork was ready to submit to the State, I was told that it would take 2 to 3 weeks to get the filed copy back. When I received it back in one week and I saw that they had received it, approved it, and filed it in only three days, I was flabbergasted! Also, I needed to have a "governing board" in place, and it turns out that the five people I asked all accepted the offer, and they each have experience and expertise in various key areas: business leadership and strategic planning, non-profit administration, non-profit development (fundraising, grant writing, and marketing), community relations, and volunteer training. So now, all the preliminary steps have been taken and all the forms have been completed. I've sent in the big packet of paperwork to the IRS, and I'm waiting for their approval. But in the meantime, many other divine connections have taken place.

The Lord has been planting seeds about working with college students who would like to do internships or volunteer work. And wouldn't you know it, "Lo and Behold" if I didn't meet a lady who works for one of the local Christian colleges. She passed my name along and now they have invited Angel Wing to become one of their community partners. So I now have two senior accounting students signed up to do their internships with me this school year and on the horizon is the opportunity to provide service learning hours to help the students meet their volunteer requirements! The representative from the College of Business specifically asked if I would be interested in having international students as interns. Oh, my goodness! Since one of my major goals is to have Angel Wing overseas at some point in the future, I felt that this was another divine connection. Plus, I recently met a lady on campus who works in the main office of the international department and guess what? She's Japanese!

I also wanted to provide Angel Wing "Birthday Blessing" visits for all of the residents at a local nursing home so that each person who lives there will receive a bouquet of flowers and a personal visit, along with a serenade of "Happy Birthday" and singing a few of their favorite hymns, and a prayer time. Well, the very first facility I asked gratefully accepted and so far it has been very well received by the residents and the staff members. In fact, I believe this is a great project to help connect the younger and older generations, so I plan to offer this as a volunteer opportunity for college students.

I've also been introduced to a young lady who is a very talented musician. She plays piano and sings and composes her own music.

31

She and I have been singing hymns with the residents at a few of the local retirement and nursing homes. We have so much in common and get along great together, like two peas in a pod. She's memorized literally hundreds of songs, many of which are the same songs I used to sing for hours when I was younger! I feel that the Lord has given me a great and wonderful gift, because as I told her, "You're like the daughter I never knew." It turns out she's also very interested in Japan and we've recently met several Japanese Christians who are also musicians and have connections with local Japanese churches. We're exploring the idea of doing some sort of music mission trips to Japan in the future!

I've told you how faithful the Lord has been to sustain us and provide for us financially through these 'lean times,' both in our family (our surprise tax refund from the IRS) and with Angel Wing (unexpected donations from local business owners and a famous country music band.) Since my vision is to expand our service area and bless even more people, I know that we will be in need of additional funds. I found out that many charities apply to receive grant money from various Foundations. I also have been investigating the numerous types of fundraising events that many not-for-profit organizations use to raise money, anything from golf tournaments to fashion shows, fancy dinners to 5-K marathons. This is definitely a whole new ballgame for me, and I'm not accustomed to hosting such large events. So for many months I had been praying about this, trying to learn more about the grant writing process and fundraising events, and asking God to send someone who could help me. Well, "Lo and Behold" a guy in one of my networking groups introduced me to his mother and guess what? ... she has lots of experience working in the fundraising and marketing departments of various non-profit agencies, and she knows how to write grants! She has kindly offered to volunteer her services and also agreed to be a member of my governing board!

As you come to the end of this chapter, my hope is that by reading my story of how God has carried me along this journey you can see the common thread running through it: "Lo and Behold" moments happen all the time! All we need to do is be watchful, patient, persistent, and obedient. I once heard a sermon in which the pastor said two things I will never forget: 1) "When God tells you to do something; you just keep doing it until He tells you to do something else," and 2) "You have to go out on a limb because that's usually where the fruit is."

When the nice gentleman who is the publisher of Light Point Press asked me to write a chapter for the book you are holding in your hands, my initial response was, "Lord, I've never written anything for publication!" and "I'm not an author!" and "I have no writing experience". So I declined the offer. Well, this gentleman is very supportive and encouraging, patient yet persistent, and he continued to ask me to write a chapter for this book. He convinced me, "people need to hear your story". So even though I felt quite overwhelmed and out of my element, I finally, although a bit reluctantly, agreed to do it. As I was sitting at the computer completing the final paragraphs, I checked my calendar and saw I had a scheduled appointment that day. I would be meeting with a nice lady whom I had met months ago at an outdoor event hosted by a local Chamber of Commerce. She had called me recently and expressed an interest in volunteering and she also wanted to learn more about the steps involved in forming a non-profit. As I was getting ready to go and meet with her, "Lo and Behold" I suddenly remembered that she is a professional editor and publisher and actually has years of experience doing this. So when we met for coffee, I just asked her if she would be willing to review what I had written, and guess what? … she graciously agreed! That is just yet another example of how the Lord provides in such marvelous and wondrous ways!

# POWER OF INSPIRATION

Jeanette Bailey is the Founder and Director of "Angel Wing Florals, Visits, & Psalms". She combines her love of flower arranging, music, and encouraging others with God's word to offer a unique visitation ministry which includes flowers and music.

Jeanette's ministry allows her the opportunity to visit people in the local hospitals, nursing homes, hospice units, retirement communities, rehabilitation facilities, Alzheimer's units, as well as private homes. She delivers flowers; and during the visit she is happy to sing hymns, read scriptures, and have a prayer time.

Jeanette holds two Bachelor's degrees, one in Secondary Education and one in Nursing. She has been a nurse for the past 16 years, working in the hospital setting and in home health. She worked as a hospice nurse for 5 years and as a school nurse for the past 7 years. She was also a choir director at a small church for several years and taught elementary music at a private Christian school for one year.

She has also had the opportunity to do mission work in Japan several times during the past 5 years. She is married and has one son. Her hobbies are gardening, singing, and playing piano.

**Jeanette Bailey, Founder & Director**
Angel Wing Florals, Visits & Psalms
501(c)(3) nonprofit organization
972-652-0636
Email: jeanette@angelwingministry.org
Website: www.angelwingministry.org

Follow Jeanette:
www.facebook.com/angelwingflorals
@_AngelWing

# POWER OF INSPIRATION

# Still Standing – After Much Heartache and Loss

By Dana D. Beard

*This chapter is dedicated to parents with personal struggles from childhood through adulthood. What children don't understand is that decisions are made based on the circumstances at hand; it is not for them to judge or be critical of even if they don't agree. Life is short - live it fully, forgive from the heart and laugh often.*

Think of your life as a work in progress … which moves us toward bliss, a sense of accomplishment, and purpose.    I grew up with childhood dreams like most teenagers and for me it was being a fashion designer by day and a private eye by night.  Wow, if I wasn't a teenager with large dreams!

As I ponder about life's challenges, I would be dishonest with myself to paint the picture that I had only experienced one – yes one – formative life event.  My dad always said that shit happens in life, and I guess in many ways he was correct.  A series of events shaped me to be who I am today: my 39 year old alcoholic mother passed away from cirrhosis of the liver in 1987; I gave birth to my first son Chancellor Allen at 18; my second child, Taylor Glenn, was born six years later when I was 24; my father—who was very tight emotionally–passed away of lung cancer in 2007. I also experienced many marriages (1-4), with just as many dogs, iguanas and cats, plus the fact that I was unable to say "no" to my children; dealt with adolescent drug and alcohol use; depression; ADD; self-medicating children unbeknownst to me; the boys' father's suicide; experiencing fight or flight in relationships; infidelity; the loss of a child; the dog chewing up my shoes; and not knowing who I was until 20 years later. Even today, in my 40s, as I take a trip back in time I recall so many struggles, unhealthy behaviors, and excessive emotional struggles with an inability to cope with my circumstances and feelings. I now know that life has meaning but I have not always felt that way. I am not crying over spoiled milk, I already did that at a young age with my mother when her sense of smell was off one morning as she prepared our cereal and though we protested at an early age. Her response to our outcry was "eat it or else." My sister, Jennifer, and I chose 'else,' waited it out and were eventually sent outside to play. Out of sight, out of mind.

Despite all the challenges in my life and the spoiled milk, there is nothing that could have prepared me for the loss of my 15 year old son, Taylor Glenn, of a brain aneurysm in January 2010. My entire world came to a crashing end. I no longer wanted to live and felt there was no life without him. The house was nothing but an empty hull without life and laughter to fill the halls. But, before we are able to focus on my personal turning point, it is important to understand the building blocks of my life.

My earliest recollection of my life's journey began over a TV dispute between my mother, Sharon, and my dad, Robert. Dad asked either me or my sister to turn the channel, mother telling my dad to get up and do it himself all the while being loaded…with alcohol. We were products of divorced parents and interestingly enough, my parents weren't. My mother was an alcoholic as was her father. Alcoholism ran in the family, and for ours, depression was also prominent. My sister and I lived with mother and her new husband and after living many years in Bossier City, LA, we moved to Waynesboro, MS, a small rural town where everyone knew someone. The funniest story was my mother's love of Coors Light's Silver Bullet. This is back when the cans had "pull tabs". She had a "pull tab" made out of old gold jewelry. And yes, it turned to the left and right just like the pull tabs on cans. I look at it today and laugh. What kind of mother does that?

There were two defining moments with my mother other than hiding her beer in the drier or having to drive at an early age because she was too drunk….or, wait for it – going to visit the Chief of Police's house so she could throw nails under his tires; and today I couldn't begin to tell you why other than she was obviously upset with the chief, and was drunk. Wow! There are so many stories with similar outcomes.

The first event occurred when I was 15, during Halloween in 1986; we were hosting a band fundraiser by creating a haunted house. It was the week before Halloween and mother dressed as a clown. I was thrilled she would be joining us because she, at times, could be a lot of fun. The alternative was she would be a mean drunk and purposely embarrass you regardless of the audience. She really went all out from the make-up to the attire; it was awesome! I recall her enjoying school events – regardless of her blood alcohol level. It was the Halloween event that mother embarrassed me so much during the haunted Halloween event that I told her I no longer wanted her to participate in my school activities. I don't recall her feelings exactly but I know it hurt or I think it did; hearing your oldest daughter say she was an embarrassment hurt her feelings but at the time, I wasn't sure she would even remember the conversation. I have never liked Halloween since.

The second event was in early 1987, when I was a junior in high school and super excited about my junior prom. I had attended several proms in years past with dates already a junior or senior but this one was MY junior class prom. I asked my mother to go with me dress shopping and was told – NO – that she was an embarrassment to me. Where do you go from there; the words had already been spoken and couldn't be taken back. I explained I didn't want her to attend school events unless she wasn't drinking and really wanted her to join me dress shopping. She did, with beer in tow! There was not a day or evening mother didn't have a beer. I found the most beautiful dress with all the accessories and couldn't wait until my prom. It was two months before prom, in 1987, and mother passed away of cirrhosis of the liver. And again, she was still the center. My prom turned out to be a drunken mess, with me following in her footsteps. Although her passing was unexpected, there was a sigh of relief…but the relief didn't come until later in life. What we learned during our formative years was how to be manipulative, lie to get what you want and to stay on mother's good side because you didn't want it the other way. Mother and her new husband had a son and was ten years younger so he didn't get to play the games we played with mother. If mother was mad at me, my sister was golden and I was ignored by both and vice versa. The silent treatment was learned at an early age and remained with us both through our adult life. I am sure she thought she was a good mother and in many ways she was but in many other ways, she wasn't. Where did we go after she passed? We went to our dad's – back to LA and our brother, Chris, went with his father.

All we knew about dad, was that he was a red-headed *explicit, explicit*. At least that is how mother described him. He lived in Louisiana at the time and was enlisted with Barksdale Air Force Base. I vaguely remember visitations until I was a teenager. There was this one period of time when my sister and I had grown tired of the situation we were buried in with mother and moved in with dad; shocker for the system that move was. His wife at the time could not have been more displeased. We were in the middle of nowhere land living on the outskirts of Shreveport off Highway 71. While with dad, mother was always pulling stunts to keep the fire burning and not in a good way! It was July or perhaps Christmas, I am not really sure. I just recall us receiving a huge box of fireworks from mother – it had to be Christmas – along with pictures of mother, and us. Stepmom was unhappy, dad was furious and all Jennifer and I thought about was getting our hands on the fireworks! Finally, we were outside on the patio, with the box of fireworks sitting on the lounger with punks lighted. We were going to town lighting up the country sky line until the "oops" came; one of us, not sure which one and it didn't matter because we were both in a world of trouble although the entire event was an accident. A lit firecracker ended up in the box of unlit firecrackers and what an unbelievable fireworks show it was...lighting up the night, one boom after another..."oops". Dad was not happy with us; but we were laughing and obviously didn't realize the seriousness of the incident until after the blaze went out. It was a quiet night after that and perhaps there was a stern call to our mother not to ever send fireworks, who really knows? This was the first time we had lived with dad; and after about a year we turned in our books and returned back to Mississippi. We realized the grass wasn't greener on the other side as thought; we were children. I recall my father telling me repeatedly, because I was deceitful and would lie over the smallest and stupidest of things, "You are going to be just like your mother and will be pregnant before you are 18." We left with that being our final words, and any other visitation with dad during my teenage years was scarce.

After mother's passing, my sister moved back to Louisiana at the beginning of the summer while I remained in Mississippi. I was entering my senior year and Jennifer was entering the 10th grade. Within that first week, dad and Jennifer were visiting family one evening and when they returned home, the current wife and her things were gone – cleaned out without even a note. I asked my sister what she did in a week to run her off! We always knew she didn't care for us, but wow, what a blow to come home and find her gone especially after losing our mother. Even though they had no children together their divorce spanned over two long years. This left our dad beyond bitter; a place we hadn't experienced with him.

41

I begged and pleaded to remain in Mississippi for my senior year, but after my summer of not being responsible, drinking and coming in at all hours of the night, dad returned to get me at the end of the summer to move me back so I could begin my senior year at Hall Summit. What I didn't learn from my mother, seriously, I learned from my dad.

Dad was not an emotional kind of guy; he loved you in his own way. For instance, he made sure we knew how to drive a stick shift and could change a tire before we could get our license. He was always there for Jennifer and me no matter how much trouble we caused. And, during my dad's watch, in early 1988, I found myself pregnant with my high school sweetheart's baby. I was scared and alone; my dad was extremely disappointed, embarrassed, and in a state of shock. Although I had many choices which were presented to me, I had a supportive father that said, "We will get through this."

I was a senior along with eight others in my class – with big dreams of immediately going off to college. After the heat subsided, I graduated Valedictorian, applied to LSUS in Shreveport and was making plans for a baby shower with an expected due date in late October. I completed 9 hours my first semester of college until my first bundle of joy arrived, October 30. He was named Chancellor Allen – Chance for short. It was the assisting nurse in the hospital that gave the "llor" to his name; a knight I recall her saying. I sat in the bed frightened, scared, crying, and wondering how on earth I was going to take care of this blessing that was going to be solely dependent upon me. It was a "chance" I was taking on both of us. Dad was the first one back in recovery, smiling from ear to ear and no longer showing signs of unhappiness; but showed signs of joy. In some ways, it was ironic that Chance was born around Halloween. It felt as though my mother was watching over us; perhaps it was her way of giving back the fun and joy to Halloween.

I knew the road would be hard, but dad taught me hard work pays off, finish school, use cash not credit, finish school, did I say that already? I went on to finish school but it spanned over the course of 15 years and many marriages.

**And, it is from here I entered my adult years and chaotic relationships.**

My first love was Richard Glenn Mangham. It was after I moved back to Louisiana, early in my senior year, that I met him at a basketball game [Small town schools didn't have football.] It was a typical whirlwind high school romance: dad didn't approve of the boy but his parents loved me so the majority of our time was spent at his house. Rick would go on to represent marriage 1 and 2. I loved him enough to marry him twice. We had a wonderful son, Chance, prior to the first marriage. I graduated high school in the spring, had Chance in the fall, and I wanted the fairytale – marry, raise our beautiful son, have house with a white picket fence, and finish my studies. Life would be grand! Rick was two years behind me in school and I was making plans for Chance and I to move to Shreveport. Yes, some have said that I took advantage of Rick while others said that I tried to control him; you decide. Dad was devastated that we moved but I felt it was time to go. I look back now and wish I had stayed at home. Perhaps things would have turned out differently. Rick and I married; he quit school, got a job and moved in with me and Chance. He later went on to obtain his GED. We had many good times but we had as many bad times when the drinking took over. We were young and jealous of each other, and when mixed with alcohol, it was one fight after another. My ideal life was not playing out like I had hoped. Having lived with an alcoholic, I didn't want the same life for my child (later to become plural.) We were mean to each other, argued and retaliated with suicide threats and it began to consume us both. We split within the first nine months of our marriage because we were headed down two different paths. From there, it was one day together and the next day apart. It was a tug of war between us, but once he committed to drinking only on the weekends, I felt like we would really have a chance. I was in no way innocent; I did my fair share of drinking, arguing and causing issues, but deep down the one thing I didn't want was a life filled with alcohol. I lived that life and knew I didn't want it for my child.

Skipping ahead a few years, it is the spring of 1994. Rick and I are together again and awaiting the arrival of our second son, Taylor Glenn, which blessed our family on April 1. What an April Fools gift from God. We were all together as a family: Rick, Chance, Taylor and I. It felt like a picture perfect family. Rick and I married a 2nd time about a month after Taylor was born. I finally had my family together. We had high hopes with dreams on the horizon to fulfill and felt like it would be achieved if we worked together. Unfortunately, to my surprise, the drinking started back in full swing. He began drinking after work with his co-workers and lying about it. On top of that weekends were always filled with friends and alcohol. I was living my childhood life all over again. Though scared and not sure how I was going to make it with two young, loving sons, I made the decision I did not want alcohol to be the center of my family especially now that we had two boys. One week before Taylor turned one, I asked Rick to leave. An unbelievable feeling came across me and I know I was scared to death but oddly I somehow knew everything in time would be better. Chance was 5 years old and Taylor had just turned 1 and I was panicked and felt that our future was uncertain. I dropped out of college, took a job with an insurance company in the fall of 1994 along with two weekend jobs, Louisiana Downs during the day and a catering position at night. My grandparents and a sitter were there to help and I was doing all I could to make it for me and the boys. We grew up together. It is funny today, and I have been picked on about it many times, but at least MawMaw Judy and I kept the boys fed. Even if it was homemade French fries and macaroni and cheese, we survived and things began to improve. Rick had moved on as had I. It was just a matter of logistics to handle having the boys every other weekend. He didn't get Taylor as much as Chance and it would play out to be a big issue between the boys later in life.

Rick's drinking didn't slow down. In fact it increased. But after the years we were able to be friends once all the court battles ended. This all coincided with husband number three but we'll get to that shortly. For now I'll focus on Rick's third divorce. He now had a litter girl with his wife and a girlfriend who had a 1-month old son by him. I am fast forwarding here but believe all of it is relevant to just what kind of life challenges I endured as well as my sons. Rick was always short on cash during this period so he would call and ask for gas or food money. It wasn't uncommon for me to take him money during my lunch break. At times we would leave the construction site for lunch while other times we'd stay on the site and talk about old times and life. Rick was jovial, charismatic and had a warm personality that drew you in!

It was the last week of July 2001 and Rick was visiting me at my apartment. His spirit was down and I could tell he wanted to share. His daughter was being kept from him and he also had issues with his current girlfriend and newborn that were weighing heavily on him. We sat on the stairs and talked and cried for hours. Rick was struggling but we managed to laugh about old times. We even had made plans for him to stay with me and the boys after his knee surgery in September because he felt he had nowhere to go. We didn't want to give the boys the wrong message, but knew that it was in his best interest to stay with us for a while. When he left he casually said, "I will call you Thursday or Friday," (which would have been August 2nd or 3rd, 2001). I didn't hear anything from Rick toward the end of the week and was rethinking the entire conversation we had earlier during the week. An uneasy feeling came over me when I couldn't reach him but there wasn't anything I could do. It was in the early morning hours of August 4th that I received a call....Rick had committed suicide. I heard the message, I know I did, but my focus was on the boys. How was I going to tell the boys? I immediately phoned my father and sister for support and my 3rd husband came to the apartment. Once dad got to the apartment, we woke up Chance and shared with him the news regarding his father. Being twelve years old, I am not sure if he truly understood what happened or not. I know he was upset but we tried to surround him with family. As for Taylor, he was a baby in my eyes. Six years old is not nearly old enough to know the word suicide so we didn't tell Taylor "why" other than his dad passed away. It would be later before Taylor knew the truth regarding the passing of his father. I had not envisioned suicide in our future.

**The man in the rain**

We were together seven years. Husband #3 was 9 years older than me and going through the most horrific divorce and custody battle with the mother of his children. It was a fiery battle that no one could imagine. His children were wonderful and, at the age I met them, you would have never thought they were part of such a tug of war. He had three children caught up in an ugly mess, an 11 year old girl and 6 year old twins, a boy and girl. Our first encounter was one night after I had pizza with friends. We had mutual friends, and while I don't think they intended our relationship to turn out the way it did, after visiting over pizza we spent several more hours talking in the rain. It was surreal. I remember a time he was at the house while the boys were spending the weekend with their father. It was Sunday and we had plans so I jumped in the shower and got out. He asked to shower and I told him he would have to take a cold one because the gas had been disconnected and I didn't have the money to turn it on. I was

46

humiliated and embarrassed. He asked about the boys' bath and I remember telling him that we would either be at MawMaw's house or I would heat water to bathe them. It certainly wasn't an ideal situation but it was all I could do at the time. The next day he paid the bill and said "do not ever let it happen again." This was someone that barely knew me. For me, I felt he was my knight in shining armor. In retrospect, I know that I was not mature enough for this relationship. Even though I felt like he was the one, I struggled with the ongoing custody battle that consumed us the entire time we were married. And when I say struggled, we all did. We had five children together and court battles brewing on both sides. It was something from a horrible novel. Unfortunately, I felt as I could not compete nor compare and was always being chastised about my whereabouts long before I spiraled out of control and wanted out. I began seeing what was out there and ended up hurting him and the children when I became unfaithful. I hurt the one man that was very much the better part of me. The summer of Rick's suicide was the summer I left husband #3. I was ashamed, embarrassed and saddened by my behavior and felt the river flowing under our bridge was too much to overcome. Our story spans over two decades, but after clearing the air years ago, we can now say that we remain close friends.

My third husband and Taylor had a relationship, and while it wasn't close, his children had taken Taylor under their wings and considered him their brother. I would be negligent if I didn't mention that during our court battle we were also fighting my ex-husband, Rick, over custody of the boys. Chance was a lovable child but had figured out at an early age how to play the games of divorced parents. He was acting out at school and every visitation with Rick would result in another hurdle. A spanking incident was at the center of my issues with their father, and for the other side as well was now over, finally. In short, Chance received a spanking and it left "a mark." Back then the slightest issue would get CPS involved. My husband and I were not declared unfit parents so Rick and his current wife lost the custody battle. My husband went on to win custody of his kids based on his work schedule but it was not without many sacrifices. Both of our exes were feeding the kids with information that kept stirring the pot rather than allowing the children to be children and have some type of a normal life – despite having divorced parents. My husband and I always had a wonderful time together, with or without the children. Many times I felt we were together but all the turmoil with exes, court dates and who gets the children when consumed our life. And I wanted more: more time together and less time battling in the courtroom. Today, I know he had no control over the situation with his ex but at the time, I felt he could have done things a little differently. I look at his 3 grown children today and have a deep love and fondness for all 3 and appreciate what they allow me to be in their lives.

The spring of 2002 I accepted a transfer to the corporate office of the insurance company I worked for. I thought that new beginnings were in order for all three of us. So, we left Shreveport and headed to Keller, TX. At the time, it was undeveloped area but I had heard wonderful things about the school district. Life was looking up for all three of us. I met a lady who had a son. He was a 'must meet' because I enjoyed golf as much as he did. After a short period, he would come to be my 4$^{th}$ marriage. It was also my last. He was everything I wasn't looking for in a husband: tattoos, alcohol with a mouth on him, but the boys loved him. The boys felt he was similar to their dad and loved the attention and fun he brought into their lives. I learned from this marriage that I would no longer settle, so I thought. He and my older son where having issues which turned into altercations and Chance gave me an ultimatum, him or me. I had always put the boys first and this time was no different. We moved on, without the husband…me, Chance and Taylor were by ourselves again.

## The Turning Point

Of all the things that the boys and I experienced, nothing prepared me for what took place in January 2010. Chance had moved out, was married with one son, Maddux Reese, and was going through his own issues. We always had a roller coaster relationship and it still exists today. When the kids were growing up I didn't say "no" enough. I allowed both boys to run over me as though I was their friend and not their mother. I should have been stronger with the discipline and stuck with the consequences. Eventually both boys turned to drugs and alcohol. Chance put us through unruly behavior and stunts. He learned from his parents that if you lie and manipulate the situation, you will normally get what you want. Taylor saw this behavior and oddly enough, was very vocal about the behaviors exhibited by Chance. They had a constant tug of war and at the root of it all was a jealousy toward one another. I wanted things to be different with Taylor. After all, there was a 6 year age difference between the boys and Chance was long gone from the house.

Taylor didn't find out that his father had committed suicide until he was in 6th grade. From that point forward Taylor began to self-medicate and act out. Not only was he diagnosed with ADD/ADHD, but he also started dealing with emotional feelings he had never experienced. We all attended grief counseling which I felt was necessary because we were all beginning to spiral out of control. Taylor's behavior was beginning to fluctuate between serious highs to lows. In 2007 when Taylor's papaw, my dad, passed away, there was a noticeable difference in Taylor. He had lost the one stable male figure in his life. He no longer was that loving child with a fun and bright personality that could keep you laughing for hours.

In 2008, I bought my first house – by myself – which would become mine and Taylor's. Taylor was with me every step of the way; even through the signing. He commented he wasn't going to do that; instead he would just take my house over when I passed. Our first night in the house was awesome. It was just the two of us with sleeping bags and peanut butter and jelly. We lay in the center of the living room talking about life, college and girls. It was a great moment between us. He was deciding rooms and felt he should have the master bedroom because I was an "old lady". I didn't think 38 was old but Taylor sure did! This didn't erase our moments of emotional issues with Taylor. He was feeling emotions he didn't quite know how to handle and was getting deeper and deeper in trouble. Taylor's depression was consuming him. We tried two separate local in-patient facilities to get him the help he needed. Eighth grade was barely completed with a passing grade. High school here we come! The 9th grade went without incident until the summer before 10th grade. Taylor was back drinking and doing drugs and needed help. He began running away if he didn't get his way. Consequences didn't seem to bother him at school or home. We had a parent meeting early in the 10th grade and I watched Taylor go off on one of his teachers. She was only trying to help; that's when I knew he was in trouble.

Due to the issues he had at school and his poor grades I began to look at other options. Our family doctor was instrumental in obtaining help for Taylor and making many "promises" to keep me alive. We had an appointment to visit a private academy; our first option. As a mom with a great love for her son, I was determined to do whatever was needed to ensure Taylor's safety and that he had a chance, and a drug free one. During our visit I recall the Headmaster asking Taylor what he would do if he had a free day to do whatever he wanted to do…and he says, "I would like to sit on the couch, smoke bud and explore." I was embarrassed but was on to what Taylor was doing because he knew it was a long shot for him to get accepted. Taylor was proud of his answer. I walked out to the waiting room to leave them alone and allow me time to cry.

I was at my wits end and the turning point was when Taylor decided to take the family car for a joy ride while I was at work. He was 15 and had no license. Now he was putting others at risk and because the police didn't see him, there was nothing to be done. I had already begun investigating other school options including inpatient facilities that would treat and provide school lessons so he wouldn't get behind. I decided on a residential treatment facility in Utah the week before Thanksgiving of 2009; I had begged and pleaded with Taylor but we weren't on the same page. I was giving him every opportunity and was getting nowhere. It was two days before Thanksgiving and all the arrangements for Taylor to attend had been made. The transport team would be at the house the next morning at 4:00 a.m. Taylor and I were sitting at the dinner table the evening before he left and Taylor said to me with tear filled eyes "I need help." He wasn't aware of the arrangements and I was doing a difficult job of holding back the tears. I explained to him that all I wanted to do was help him get the treatment necessary. It is in the wee hours of the morning and the transport team had arrived. Taylor's suitcase was already packed per the instructions on the intake form. I was to wake him up, tell him I love him and walk out of the room…easy right? No! Taylor popped up out of bed as though he knew what was going on, told me he loved me and asked if he could brush his teeth before leaving. My stomach was empty and my heart was breaking. I was contacted when they made it to the airport and was told he was the most cordial child and had already spilled the beans on everything he had done and put us through; and I wept.

My heart was broken thinking about him being miles away with only letters to communicate until he earned points. We wrote weekly and it included many apologies and many "I love you's." By December Taylor was caught up with his 10th grade studies, was doing well and completing his weekly quote that would rack up points for him which would allow us a phone call. Taylor was even writing about college. I was super excited because he wanted to attend the University of North Texas. He was proud when I graduated college. I was turning 40 in March and Taylor was doing everything he could to earn enough points because he wanted to talk with the "old lady."

It is the eve of January 18, and I was out of town on business. I received a call from the school that no parent ever wants to hear, "Something has happened, you need to get here." Even when I asked for clarification, all I could get was that Taylor had been rushed to the hospital. I was finally able to speak with a doctor and I asked, "He's ok, right?" It is a blur today. I phoned a dear friend that arranged my flight for first thing in the morning to Las Vegas, Nevada. The school officials were with Taylor at Sunrise Children's Hospital and picked me up at the airport. I had tons of questions for the school officials that picked me up however they didn't have an answer other than the doctor is waiting on you.

Upon my arrival to the hospital, I was praying to God this was all a mistake; that Taylor was fine. The doctor said "brain aneurysm" and I didn't understand. "He will be ok, right?" I wasn't hearing what the doctor said…and I kept saying he will be ok, Taylor is a fighter. It was shortly thereafter the doctor said "Taylor is on life support; he is brain dead." We brought him back twice however he has no brain function. How? I don't understand…did someone hit him…did he fall? The doctor said if Taylor had been on the steps of the hospital, there was nothing they could have done to save him. The brain aneurysm ruptured. What brain aneurysm? My goodness, all of the questions I was asking and still not understanding what just happened to my Taylor. Taylor passed away January 19, 2010. The decision was made to donate many of his organs to provide life to others.

How does a parent lose a child? Why would God allow such a thing to happen; especially to a young man who had finally turned a corner and put in his last letter, "mom, for the first time in my life, I feel like a normal child." Why wasn't Taylor allowed the opportunity to live life, drug free and happy for probably the first time in his life? I was angry and didn't agree with the choice God had just made for us.

## The change

I was empty throughout 2010 and 2011. I had been clinically diagnosed with PTSD and Major Depressive Disorder. It felt more secure staying in my room letting the world pass me by. School years passed and I purposely avoided the stores because I didn't want life to move on without Taylor. How could parents be happy with school starting when I no longer had Taylor? People were telling me, it is time to get over it and move on. How do you do that or where is the book on moving on after the loss of a child? "What idiots," I thought; for some people to have all the answers while having no experience of losing a child. This would be the turning point of my life. My therapist was my life savior – she taught me how to set boundaries and stick with them to protect me. She taught me how to take care of myself first.

During this time I decided to promote the Brain Aneurysm Foundation. Since Taylor's passing I spent most of my time researching what brain aneurysms were and how to detect them. I pulled together the energy to hold two walks as memorials to Taylor and to raise money for brain aneurysm awareness. But instead of having a sense of fulfillment it was just a painful reminder of my loss.

It is 2012, two and a half years later, and I am trying to figure out my life's next steps. I created the Taylor Mangham Foundation and was able to raise the funds to give away two scholarships to Keller High School Students (this was the year which Taylor would have graduated) which was a great joy being able to help students fulfill their dream of college. But I knew my journey of helping wasn't going to stop there. During a random day in March this year a friend shared with me about a position with the National Alliance on Mental Illness (NAMI) of Tarrant County. They were looking for a Walk Manager. I tossed the idea around a bit and decided to submit my resume. From there, it unfolded and I have been active ever since. It brings me great pleasure when I speak about NAMI Tarrant County or my own personal struggles and afterwards people share with me their own personal stories. At times there are tears, laughter, and talks of hope. It is the hope that I hold on to today. Hope that tomorrow will be better than today. Hope that I will get out of bed and accomplish one thing that touches someone's life. Hope that I have a forgiving heart for those not mature enough to understand what it is like to lose a child and the ability to forgive those that judge me. I recognize that life is short and we should live each moment as if it was our last, and today I can honestly say I know from the heart what that means. I keep Taylor's favorite quote close to my heart, "What we do for ourselves dies with us. What we do for others and the world remains and is immortal" – Albert Pine.

I know we are all God's children, on loan and only He has the plan. And everyone experiences loss but no parent should ever have to bury their child; it is against the natural flow of life. I speak out today because if my story and that of my life journey as an individual, mother and wife helps one person or a family, then I made a difference.

Dana D. Beard is a native of Louisiana and has lived in Keller, Texas since 2002. Dana has been an employee of a managing general agency since 1984, where she started as a data entry assistant and worked her way to Director of Human Resources. While working full-time and raising two wonderful sons, Dana graduated with a BA in Insurance at the University of North Texas. After the tragic passing of her youngest son to a brain aneurysm, Dana conducted various fundraisers for the Brain Aneurysm foundation. While working with her state representative, she successfully passed a resolution declaring September as Brain Aneurysm Awareness month in Texas.

As a survivor of her life's circumstances, Dana also speaks out with courage and a strong will to anyone who needs encouragement and support. Her mission is to change lives, one at a time. Dana has personally experienced mental illness since the death of her son and is now working toward educating individuals that have misconceptions or do not understand the cause and effects of mental illnesses. She is determined to stomp out the stigma associated with mental illness.

Today, Dana is a nonprofit advocate who has committed herself to building the capacity of the National Alliance of Mental Illness in Tarrant County as their Director of Public Relations. She works to strengthen the organization by hosting events, workshops and other learning opportunities that serve the community. Dana is currently working on two books that depict life experiences that most people will endure but very few will openly speak about.

**Dana D. Beard**
Website: www.danabeard.com
Website: www.nami.org
Email: namitc.beard@gmail.com
Email: theone@danabeard.com

<u>Follow Dana</u>
www.facebook.com/NAMItarrant
www.facebook.com/dana.beard
@TheOneDanaBeard
@NAMITC1

# Life of Choices, Life of Change

By Kimberly Cantergiani

*"I don't know how I would have made it through the roughest of times without Rob, Marshall and Maurice. When everything else is falling apart, I dance until I collapse in exhaustion, lie in bed and weep or workout furiously. Music has the power to transform my soul, renew my spirit and silence my brain. I owe my foundational attributes and character to a richly diverse heritage of warriors who never retreated when it came to love or principle. Finally, I am most indebted to things 1 through 6 for providing intense and varied opportunities to be honed into something significantly better than I was and who continue to be my very best friends."*

We all have those moments. Moments which rob us of our ability to feel whole, rational and sane. Moments that cause us to question everything we thought we knew and the relevance of our meager existence. Moments of anger, and even rage, at how we arrived where we are. Moments paralyzed by fear that we aren't good enough and the belief that nothing we do will change anything. Soon, those moments become hours, then days and then weeks. We go on, as Thoreau said, to "live lives of quiet desperation."

Fewer, and perhaps more fleeting, are moments of insight and clarity. Moments that glimmer with the hope of all that could be. Moments that tease us with the notion that we were destined for something more. Moments that whisper that you are not only good enough, but you are amazing beyond compare. Moments that resonate "YOU ARE A UNIQUE CREATION, UNRIVALED THROUGHOUT ALL OF HUMANITY!!!"

Sadly, we rarely stack these moments the way we do the others. But should we, a broad expanse is revealed and we become intimately aware of our unlimited potential for change. The choice is ours, and the choice is now. The past is gone. The present is merely a representation of all that has come before. And the future...well, the future is wide open with possibility. The future is sculpted by the choices we make now. We, alone, are entirely responsible for who and what we become.

If someone had said this to me "back then" (and someone probably did), I had a long list of stories I told to substantiate my lot in life. They were colorful and varied and some were even true. Did you ever stop to think that maybe the stories we tell ourselves aren't? I certainly didn't. Nor did I consider the possibility that living in the past and feeling stuck by current circumstances was not allowing me to create a future without more of the same. However, when I came to realize the power inherent in choice, and the freedom it provides, I was finally able to break free of self-imposed limitations and begin building the life of my dreams. And if I can do it, so can you.

After 10 pregnancies and the births of six children, I found myself in the summer of 2000 fat, tired, and depressed. Life had provided an endless series of deviations from my original plan. Reality did not come anywhere close to my imagined utopia for I felt as though a giant vacuole had formed in my earth that engulfed me partially, like descending in quicksand, but never entirely swallowed me whole.

The crumbling of my first marriage, with incidents of verbal and physical abuse, drug and alcohol consumption and infidelity, devastated me. Alone at 20, with two children and a 10th grade education, I was ill-equipped to manage life, but I did the best I could. I worked hard to provide stability for my children, despite the gut-wrenching ache that gnawed at me continuously about the unfairness of it all. I knew I was a good person and had always tried to do the right thing; how could this be happening to me?

Nonetheless, I persevered and over the next few years I found myself surviving, but not thriving. Then I met a man at church and was intrigued by his willingness to accept my situation; divorce, single parenthood and all, and we began dating. His commitment to being chaste until we were married seemed to seal the deal and we were married the following year. Unfortunately, while these were wonderful qualities, enough time had not been spent to adequately assess compatibility and the congruence of foundational beliefs and values.

A decade later I could no longer deny that we were living a functional business relationship. Not only was it without friendship and passion, but our differences were magnified as we attempted to raise children together. He was in denial about the problems, unwilling to engage in solution-focused dialogue or consider counseling and things continued to escalate. There was no doubt my marriage was falling apart.

Concurrently, two of my kids were using drugs and were constantly in trouble with the law and another had profound ADHD. I am not talking about the kind of ADHD that everyone is so quick to diagnose these days when a perfectly healthy kid just needs some activity instead of sitting in front of a TV or at a desk all day. I am talking about a kid who literally could not sit still, follow any task to completion or fall asleep at night. I felt like life was just crashing in around me. I would say I was suicidal, except that wasn't even an option. As bad as it was, I couldn't imagine who would take care of things if I was gone, so my death was off the table as far as options went.

I am always impressed by the human capacity for seeking coping mechanisms. In an effort to fill the holes, we become addicted to alcohol, drugs, cigarettes, sex, power, people, sleep, shopping and more. For me, eating had become far more than fuel for a complex living organism; it had evolved to a state of significant emotional gratification. Late at night, the solace of silence marked the end of another grueling day, and time was my own. This was the only refuge I felt I had from the responsibilities to my family and the only time I didn't have to be concerned about someone else's needs. I indulged in whatever I happened to be craving at the time.

Feelings of joy dissipated quickly, for even before the last bite had been ingested, self-loathing and disgust occupied their regular seats in my mind. At 5'3", I had ballooned to 191 lbs. and showed no signs of slowing. At the time, I related the horrid perceptions of myself as an incompetent and useless person incapable of any minor self-restraint to my obesity, but much later I learned that, in truth, they were primarily due to my having lost control over myself and my life.

My "salvation" began in an unlikely and arbitrary location: La Plaza Mall. Lugging around almost 200 lbs. on a short, small frame was no minor task though, for I became winded easily. I sat on a short, metal bench, waiting for my son, biding my time with a pretzel and cream cheese, nonchalantly surveying the crowd yet avoiding eye contact at all costs. If you knew me now, you would likely find this hard to believe. Once timid and shy, presently I am anything but. It was during this panoramic sweep of my immediate surrounding that the display in the bookstore caught my eye.

Through the glass enclosure, I could make out the coverlet, which clearly depicted some major weight loss claims. After a minor hesitation, I entered the threshold and retrieved the manuscript, Body-for-LIFE, and studied the photographs, which documented magnificent physical progress in twelve weeks.

Scanning the content, I warily assessed the outline of a program designed for "mental, spiritual and physical change." Topics covered included goal-setting, motivational techniques, nutrition and exercise instructions. While the plan appeared to be sound and reasonable, I had my reservations. At that juncture, I had Weight Watch-ed, Jenny Craig-ed, vegetarian-ed, Atkins-ed and Rotated. I was leery of another endeavor that might leave me more emotionally fatigued than I was when I began. Just beyond the store exit, I was propelled back inside by a desperate impulse to make the purchase.

The following thirty-six hours found me mostly in bed, devouring the text, the message of encouragement gaining rapid credibility. Along with the photographs, the book is brimming with testimonials written by people who had experienced something far more than just a physical transformation. These people had transformed their lives! Their stories of overcoming alcohol abuse, family death, debt, sickness, bad jobs, and relationships. A strong ribbon of victory and triumph was woven throughout the message of the book, but unlike many other motivational texts included answers for practical application.

The resonating invitation from the author compelled me. A challenge, in the form of a national contest, is extended as a motivational force, intended to drive the reader to personal success. So, I gathered, from the shambles of my spirit, the few remaining scraps of desire, and began to implement the program as outlined in the book. I managed to locate some reservoir of strength, and with fervor and zeal, set out to win.

I quickly determined that my tendency toward caring for others before myself, while not an entirely negative quality, could be a stumbling block. Since I had learned and come to believe that knowing your weaknesses could be helpful, I devised a plan for coping and navigating in order to reach my final destination. I decided to sponsor a "Pound-A-Thon" to benefit the local battered women's shelter. Requesting donations and pledges from everyone I knew ensured that I would not be able to quit easily and that I was asked about my progress everywhere I went.

I prepared a binder to help me through the twelve-week course which included training logs, meal plans, schedules, "before" pictures, elaborately detailed goals and self-promises, deadlines and photos of the kind of physique I dreamed of for myself. I summarized an emotionally charged testament to the incredible feelings that I would experience at the attainment of my goals, which I cemented in my brain mentally by reading aloud at least twice each day.

I wrote to Bill Phillips, owner of EAS and the sponsor of the Body-for-LIFE Challenge, detailing my binder and encouraging him to create a "success journal" for other BFLers. A few weeks later I received a phone call from his assistant, Amy, inquiring about the details of my binder and a year later the spiral bound, Body for Life Success Journal was published with my feature on Day 62. While this was not a profound victory for me personally, it is indicative of one of those moments when you observe some positive result from choosing to take action.

I slowly made manageable changes to my nutritional program (not DIET!), exercised six days each week, alternating weight training with cardiovascular exercise and persevered regardless of how I felt. This sounds pretty straight-forward, right? What many do not know is that throughout the first three or four weeks, I left the gym each morning crying and vowed I would never return again. People who have never been out of shape do not realize how hard it is to enter that public arena when you are not part of the fit crowd or how being that tired and sore affects you every moment of every day until your body adjusts.

First of all, I was paranoid and self-conscious. I thought everyone was staring at the fat lady who couldn't stay on the treadmill for more than eight minutes. Second, it did not escape my awareness that significant social activity was taking place; business people networked and the typical male-female pursuits were in full force, including the staff. I couldn't even get the people who worked there to answer my questions about how to use the equipment. Finally, a complete lack of coordination and strength caused me to stumble and move awkwardly. Once I even fell off the bench! All of these combined made every morning a challenge in more ways than one.

Re-reading my goals throughout the day was the only thing that kept me on course. I had a detailed and graphically visual description for precisely what I wanted to look and feel like at the completion of my twelve week challenge and I regularly took time in my day to sit still and close my eyes and fully focus on the end result as if it had already happened. I felt my flat stomach and firm thighs. I felt the energy, confidence and joy. I smelled the ocean air and heard the seagulls while I played with my kids at the beach. I got tears in my eyes picturing Bill Phillips bringing me my big check, champion jacket and diamond ring.

Quickly, lack of coordination was replaced as my muscles developed and I became more comfortable and confident about what I was doing. Persistence proved itself to be correlated to results and slowly, my body began to change. There were small changes at first; I wasn't winded after climbing a flight of stairs and could carry more grocery bags in one trip. I felt energized, began to enjoy rising early and found that I had clarity of mind. I pressed forward and became more excited with each day about the changes that were taking place in my body and my life. I studied fitness and nutrition but also became a devoted student of human behavior and began reading everything I could get my hands on in the fields of positive psychology, personal development and peak performance.

This is where things got really exciting. I learned that the things successful people do, and do consistently, apply to every facet of life. The formula for success can be applied by anyone who wants to make a change in any area of their life. As I learned to relinquish control over what was not mine and focused only on what was within my power, I discovered I held the key to unlocking my potential. Self-mastery in one area was contagious and quickly spread to all facets of my life.

I began to enjoy my children in a way that I had never experienced before. I had energy and desire to play with them. Along with the fun came talking and open, honest communication on many levels. I learned to address challenging and uncomfortable issues in mature and rational ways. Simply, yet profoundly, the children began to exhibit control over their lives and learned to own their behaviors and accept natural consequences.

At the completion of three consecutive Body-For-Life Challenges, I had lost over 70 lbs., wore a size 0 and had a body-fat measurement of 10.5%. This was a radical departure from the size 22W and 40.3% body-fat when I began! The physical changes ended up being the "icing on the cake." What had begun as a weight-loss odyssey became a soul transformation affecting everyone within my influence. Thoughts of the contest on the backburner, I knew I had already won, accomplishing more than I had ever dreamed possible. However, in March 2002, I was notified that I had won the title of 2001 Body-for-LIFE Grand Champion, which included $25,000, a luxurious Western Caribbean cruise and an endorsement contract.

By that time, I had already faced my fears and insecurities and gained the courage to end my marriage and moved out on my own with the four children remaining at home, despite the fact that I didn't have a job or education. Lots of smart folks would probably have chosen to stay awhile to make a plan, secure a job, save some money or go back to school. But once I knew there was no hope for growth in the marriage, staying just felt like living a lie. So I took the kids and our personal belongings, leaving the house, furniture and appliances behind and committed to re-inventing a new life for me and the kids.

We moved into a two bedroom apartment, two sets of bunk beds in one room and one in the other with a small living area between. I did a little temporary work for a few months and quickly realized new aspects of my personality. A combination of an entrepreneurial spirit, passion for helping others and what had become an obsession with health and fitness resulted in personal trainer certification, eventually followed by opening a private fitness studio. Within a little time, I was able to develop additional income streams with corporate wellness programs, nutrition packages, professional speaking and life coaching. I enjoyed wonderful success, built a custom home, bought a new car and started taking vacations. Life was good! I would love to report that we all lived happily ever after, but as you know, regardless of whatever progress we've made, life continues to throw curve balls; those moments where everything gets blurry and in which the choices we make inevitably create our destiny.

I was working with a client on May 22, 2006, the night before my 39th birthday when I felt numbness and tingling in my right leg similar to what we call "falling asleep". I shook it out a little and stretched before I went to bed. The next morning I woke up completely unable to move. There was no position I could roll or move into that did not result in excruciating jolts throughout my body like what I can only imagine being electrocuted feels like, though I have never been. A friend drove me to an orthopedic surgeon which, in and of itself was quite a feat as I couldn't bend at the waist or legs at all. I soon learned that I had suffered a significant back injury.

My lower back was broken, almost in a straight horizontal line and I had ruptured disc L5, S1. Not that it mattered at that point, but no one could tell me how. Sometimes these things are just an accumulation of strain and pressure that finally snapped. Business slowed, and eventually halted, as I was laid up for over six months. Intensive research deterred me from having the surgery that was recommended as everyone I interviewed expressed, at best, marginal relief and, at worst, exacerbated problems. I worked with a variety of holistic practitioners for pain management, yet the final prognosis was that it was simply a matter of time before I ended up in a wheelchair.

In retrospect, I see that being in this position provided another one of those moments that demanded a choice that required me to set my fears aside, as real and profound as they were, and attempt to move in a forward direction. I sold my house and car, moved into a two bedroom apartment AGAIN, bought a 20 year old vehicle and went back to school to get that magical piece of paper that gets you entrance into the business world.

As mentioned previously, I left high school in the $10^{th}$ grade, so returning to academia was no simple task. Despite high entrance exam scores, I was required to attend a community college first, which was fine with me because I was scared to death to go back to school and this allowed me a smaller campus and class sizes. Words cannot express how phenomenal the experience was for me. The excitement of learning at a time in my life where I was ready and willing to apply myself was incredible. I was surprised to enjoy interesting relationships with both faculty and new cohorts half my age and even more surprised when I won the Presidential Inspirational Achievement Award and was invited as a commencement speaker. When the time came to receive my Associate's degree in Biology and move to the University, it was bittersweet.

Personal training combined with my injury made the body a natural area of study for me and I went on to receive my Bachelor's degree in Pre-Med Biology with a minor in Chemistry. I graduated with a 3.8 GPA, was a member of both Phi Theta Kappa and Golden Key

International Honor Societies and was listed in Who's Who Among Students in American Colleges and Universities. I ardently pursued entrance to medical and graduate school and was concurrently accepted to two programs, both requiring relocation. While this involved even more moments of risk and uncertainty, to do nothing would still be a choice. After weighing all the options we moved to Fort Worth, Texas in May of 2011 just ten days following graduation and a week before my new program began. This particular choice proved to carry some substantial fallout. While my two teens were supportive of the move for my academic goals, none of us really knew what that would entail.

My 15 year old daughter developed a bleeding ulcer from internalizing her stress over the relocation. She hadn't shared the pain she was experiencing with me because she was trying to allow me to follow my dreams. I was devastated to realize my decisions may have not been calculated enough. She had always been pretty social and outgoing, so I had not considered the realities for a teenager in a new school and with the loss of her supportive peer group. To make matters worse, three months into my studies I realized I was miserable. I was only sleeping about four hours each night, hardly saw my kids and I couldn't even keep up with the ones who didn't live with me!

I realized I needed to get back to doing what I love, which is helping people transform their lives from where they are to where they want to be and truly unlocking their potential so that they can be achieving success, whatever that means to them. Regardless of the places the roller coaster of life has taken me, I am grateful for being able to live life to the fullest and live without regrets. I firmly believe that every choice and experience has contributed to the person I am today and are what give me the ability to motivate and inspire others, as well as share techniques for harnessing individual potential and power.

In January I ceased medical studies and have instead re-built my speaking and coaching business. I am also a graduate student at UT

Dallas where I will earn my MBA with an emphasis on Organizational Behavior and Executive Coaching and am preparing for certification as an NLP practitioner.

When I think about my life, all that has transpired and changes that have come as a result of powerful choices, it all seems very remarkable. At the same time, I recognize that I am very ordinary. I do not possess some unique, super-human quality that allowed me to rise above circumstances and obstacles. Many people have been through far greater challenges than I. Yet the very same things separate those who are living in the flow, designing the life of their dreams and those who are not – the choices we make, the attitude we bring, the meaning we attach to our experiences and the ability to take 100% responsibility for who and what we will be.

There is really nothing fundamentally different between who I used to be and who I am now, nor is there between me and you. We are all living lives replete with moments that present us with unlimited possibilities, and it is up to us to create a vision of our dream life and cast a laser-like focus on bringing it to pass, foregoing our love affair with mediocrity and blame of external circumstances. You are eternal in nature and possess all of the resources within yourself to have, be or do anything you set your mind to. And if I can do it, *anyone* can.

Kim Cantergiani is an expert in human behavior and transformation and combines that with her experience in overcoming obstacles to help people live their highest vision and accelerate their path to success. She helps close the gap from where they are to where they want to be.

With a passion for helping clients, audience participants and coaching members move past the PAST, leverage CHANGE and put real world strategies in place – it's no wonder her clients call her "Unstoppable!"

Kim has worked with hundreds of clients to clarify vision and create focused plans for going from "good" to "great", and from "great" to "outstanding".

She is featured in Muscle Media, Energy & People magazines as well as the national best-sellers, Body-for-LIFE for Women and the Body-for-LIFE Success Journal. She has also been a featured writer in RGV Woman, Health & Fitness Source, Pulse and Vision magazines.

**To learn more about bringing Unstoppable Kim to your next event, contact her via phone or email.**

**Kim Cantergiani**
KC International
817-269-0952
Email: kim@kimcantergiani.com
Website: www.KimCantergiani.com

Follow Kim:
www.facebook.com/kdcantergiani
Twitter: @KimCantergiani

# Yes You Can

By Reggie Carney

*I dedicate this project to Almighty God; my creator, sustainer and ultimate coach. He created me to make a difference and I'm excited that he's afforded me yet another opportunity to do so. I also want to dedicate this project to my Wife, Nature, my daughters, Nadia and Naiya and my parents; I don't know where I would be without their love, support and encouragement.*

Imagine this for a moment!  You're a sophomore in high school.  10<sup>th</sup> grade!  You are a popular, well-liked kid.  You are an excellent student and a star athlete on the basketball and football teams.  You have excellent relationships with classmates, teachers, coaches and administrators alike.  You are well-respected by your classmates-not only for your athletic abilities, but also for your academic excellence. You are so highly regarded by your classmates that, unbeknownst to you, they nominate you sophomore class president.  Wow.  Imagine that!  So unexpected, was this nomination!  Upon hearing the news, you are in a state of disbelief, but enthusiastically excited and proud that they see something valuable in you.  The excitement shows all over your face.  You confidently stroll the corridors with your head held high, proud that your classmates think so highly of you.  You're popular and capable in their eyes; does anything else matter to a sophomore in high school!  Your glow is blinding; causing people to stop to see what's up with you.  Wouldn't that have been an awesome experience!  Let's continue…

Well, in the midst of all the excitement, there is something you failed to understand about this nomination. The magnitude of this small, overlooked detail would likely change your entire outlook of just how *great* this nomination really is; therefore dimming the blinding glow that everyone has noticed.

The news: you've got to deliver a campaign speech as a part of your candidacy. And, you're charged with delivering this speech to the entire student body. Whoa! What's your first thought? What's your initial emotion? What's your next action? I can answer all these questions and more, because this is my story. It happened over 25 years ago, back at West High School in Wichita, Kansas.

My response, to the news about the campaign speech! Well, I thought, "Oh crap!" I felt an intense terror, along with a shortness of breath. Yes, I struggled to breathe. I completely froze with fear. I was a deer looking into headlights. This was my thought progression: Deliver a speech to the sophomore class -- scary, but doable. Deliver a speech to the sophomore and junior class -- more scary but doable. But deliver a speech to the entire student body -- *NO WAY!* This was the scariest scenario! I was overwhelmed! I had no exposure and no experience speaking publicly. I was a reserved kid back then. Although known as a prankster at home, I wasn't at all outgoing in public. I can never remember being as afraid as I was in that moment.

My fear of public speaking was anchored in 3 primary areas. First, it was an issue of competence. I knew nothing about delivering a speech. I had never done it before and didn't know the first step involved in carrying out the task. I didn't have people offering to help me create and practice delivery, and I was either, too proud or too scared to ask for help. I was completely vulnerable!

Second, I believe my fear was an issue of confidence. I didn't realize this back then, but everything I had become good at, had taken time. Because of the work I had invested, certain things had become easy and somewhat effortless. Playing sports, working on bicycles and installing car stereos were all effortless. They didn't require much thought. Instinctive is the word that comes to mind. Today, I know my confidence had developed over time.

I didn't have this same confidence with creating and delivering speeches. And it makes perfect sense today; I just had not done it before. Now I see I hadn't always been good at those other things either. Early attempts at basketball and football, I'm sure were not pretty. I was unconsciously incompetent where speeches were concerned; I didn't know what I didn't know and the result was pure and absolute fear.

Finally, I can't ignore the issue of my reputation. What would everyone think when I flopped? Everyone thought so highly of me. It would be an "ALL EARS ON ME" experience as I delivered the speech over the intercom. Oh, did I forget to mention the speech was delivered over the intercom? Didn't matter one bit, I was still petrified! As I said earlier, I was well-known in my school: a pretty popular kid, and a respected student-athlete. I was likeable. And for these reasons, I had everything to lose!

Bottom line for me (in my 15 year-old mind) I had a reputation to uphold. And, there was no way to fail safely in this moment. My failure would be public; in front of the entire student body. No matter the confidence I projected in other settings, I cared about what people thought of me. I was athletic and smart, but deep down I was insecure and self-conscious. And, I didn't really know how to deal with public failure. Botching that speech meant facing brutal classmates and the ridicule that is so prevalent with that age and stage. They would now see a crack in my armor; so I thought. What a heavy burden for a fifteen-year-old kid…wouldn't you say?

So, upon hearing the news of the speech, I gasped as I tried to digest the reality of the situation. It totally caught me off-guard. No longer was I able to focus in class. No longer was I the sharp shooter on the basketball court. No longer was I as loose and playful with close friends and family. Why! Because the cloud of that darn speech overwhelmed the living daylight out of me. I was freaked out! It was a very dark time in my life! I was on the cusp of making a fool of myself in front of the entire school. They would know the *real* Reggie…not the calm, cool and collected leader they had come to know. Can you feel the gravity of the situation! I need you to *feel* what I was feeling in that moment.

I was a basket case the days and weeks leading up to the speech. Numb is probably a good way of describing my state of mind.

I remember listening to other candidates delivering their speeches. They seemed so eloquent. Candidates laid out their speeches so nicely; their qualifications, their vision, and the value they could bring to the presidency. Whoa! With every speech I heard, as you can imagine, I became more and more deflated and discouraged. I told no one of my fear. I internalized all this anxiety. It was awful…"Why me", I thought! Now that I think about it, I could have had a heart attack.

To make a long story bearable (as my friend and coach Nate Brooks says), my time had arrived. I remember making my way to the office; knees trembling, expression blank, and a cloud of doubt and uncertainty hanging over my head. I had not prepared a speech, so I had no idea what I would say. I just knew people expected me to deliver; and I always had. I have no idea how I even made it to the office that day. I walked in the office during the conclusion of another candidate's speech. I was up next! There was a very brief introduction by the assistant principal, and then he handed that old-style standup microphone to me. My heart was racing.

I tentatively grasped the microphone with much trepidation. I paused for a moment and I delivered my *entire* speech. Yes, I actually did it! I made it through the whole speech. No preparation and no practice! It was amazing. The only problem was my speech consisted of three whole words: "**VOTE FOR ME!**" Yep, it happened just like that; no kidding. I was done and I was out of there!

Unbelievable huh? That was my campaign speech and my first exposure to public speaking. When audiences hear this story and especially the punch line, their expressions are priceless and the laughter uncontrollable. Jokes, tying back to the speech, persist throughout the session. We laugh together. They can't believe it! Truthfully, I couldn't believe it either. In the moments following the speech, all I could say was "I'm glad it's over."

I tell this story a lot. After the story, the first question is always the same; "Did you win?" Early on, I would say I won, with a long pause, then I would say second place. I would pause again and say out of two candidates. They'd laugh! Today, thanks to a wise lady in one of my presentation skills sessions, I now say "There are two answers to that question." I tell them, while Ramona, my 4.0 GPA classmate who graduated top of our class, won the election for the presidency; I also won! I did indeed win because I delivered it; I stepped up, faced my fear and delivered the speech. This is what that lady in New Jersey told me. I didn't have to go through with it! I could have remained in my comfort zone; keeping my reputation in-tact...at least for a *little* while longer. Never would I have imagined that over 25 years later, I would be speaking, presenting and facilitating for a living. I'm amazed!

Here's the question: Why is the fear of public speaking so debilitating...so terrifying for so many of us? In my travels, I run into so many people who struggle with the same overwhelming fear with which I once struggled. Interestingly, many of these people are high-level professionals and even executives. I hear it all the time, "I could never do what you do." They go on to tell me how afraid or uncertain they are and what happens to them at the thought of having to speaking publicly.

I'll never forget this technical executive in Virginia. He said, "I would rather be on fire than to speak in front of people." Can you sense the intensity of that fear? This is about the time I tell them, "Yes You Can!" which is where the name of my upcoming book comes from. After asking a few questions, I will tell them (If I haven't already) where my journey began and perhaps a few other challenges that I've faced. I've appropriately named these stories, my not-so-glory stories. The reality of my situation is that I'm an engineer by degree. I'm a recovering perfectionist. I truly struggled with this skill. This was not an easy journey for me.

I get so much mileage from my not-so-glory stories because they encourage and give people hope. Once I begin to tell about the struggles and challenges, what seemed impossible for them, all of a sudden seems possible. I see a new found hope in their eyes. They don't see me as this guy who was born with a gift and is effortlessly operating in his gift. They now see a journey; a path; a process at work over many years.

"But how did you do it?" they ask. In many cases, well-meaning people expect a quick answer; a quick fix. I did this or I did that and...*poof!* I'm sure there are those out there who experienced success that way; almost instantly. That's not the norm and it's not my story. I tell them it took years for this process to work fully for me. In fact I heard Dr. John Maxwell say it took him over 7 years to sharpen his public speaking skills.

While I may give them a couple of tips or tell them a story or two, I let them know that for me it was a long arduous journey; *journey* being the key word. Again, this may not be the case for everyone, especially if you grew up in an environment where public speaking was common-place or if you have one of those outgoing personalities with a gift for gab and the stage. Not my situation! For the rest of us, it simply takes longer. But, it's possible!

I truly believe if we don't face this fear early, it intensifies. It gets worse! We begin to worry more and more about irrelevant matters that impede the process of growth. I'll explore this issue more in my book. I don't underestimate the opportunity I had to face this fear at 15 years of age. Fifteen years old is still late, but I still consider myself fortunate.

There *is* hope for those of you who struggle with silencing the fears that make speaking publicly seem impossible. I love the message that Malcolm Gladwell shares in his book *What the Dog Saw* where he celebrates "late bloomers." In our society we've become so intrigued with child prodigies; those who get a fast start. "Precocity" Gladwell calls it. Picasso is one of Gladwell's examples of precocity. Picasso peaked at age 21 or 22. Cezanne, another well-known artist, was one of Gladwell's examples of a late-bloomer. Cezanne peaked in his 50's and 60's. I see myself as a late-bloomer. I didn't get a fast start. I didn't peak early as a public speaker.

If we're not careful though, discouragement can set in. If we find we're not keeping pace with our contemporaries, we think something's wrong. The reality is *nothing's* wrong; *absolutely* nothing! We don't all develop at the same pace, and that's perfectly normal. For many of us, it just takes longer. The trick is to focus on our *own* journey; our *own* path; our *own* route. Carol Dweck, psychologist and professor at Stanford University, in her book Mindset writes about what she calls the "growth mindset." This mindset is all about becoming. It's about growing; about progress and process. She contrasts this "growth" mindset with what she calls the "fixed" mindset. This "fixed" mindset is about perfection. It's about being. It's about natural giftedness and intellect.

The purpose of this snippet (along with my upcoming book) is to encourage you. Zig Ziglar says to everyone who comes through his Monday-Morning Devotion "You should write a book." "You have a message…You have a purpose…You have a story that someone needs to hear." He goes on to say "If you fill your book with encouragement, it'll sell." We all need encouragement! One of his great quotes is "Encouragement is the *fuel* on which hope runs." I want to be the one that tells you, *YOU CAN*! I want to affirm you and build you up. You *can* speak publicly. Even beyond public speaking, whatever it is you want to do, *YOU CAN*! It doesn't matter where you're starting from; *YOU CAN*! You just have to get started. Initially, it might resemble a three-word campaign speech, but you never know what will come of it; you just have to take the first step.

As I recount my story in the book, I share key principles discovered on my journey. I use *R.O.U.T.E.* as an acronym (a model) to guide the experience. I use each letter in ROUTE to highlight a key action I took on my journey. Each action aligns with a 'Rule-of-the-Road' (a principle) necessary for achieving success. Finally, I link these principles to leadership, showing the universal application of the principles to achieving success in any area.

I chose this acronym because it fits nicely with my metaphor for life; Life's a journey. I believe we're all on a journey to fulfill a predefined purpose. The model also fits with my belief that we all have different paths to fulfilling our purpose.

Whether you are facing a fear of public speaking, starting a business, writing a book, or working at success in a relationship, the model works to help you achieve success. You'll surely have different challenges to overcome. Your struggles will likely be unique. Your path will have its own trajectory and terrain. Whatever your situation, you may find a tip or a truth to help enhance your own journey. This is the universal application of which I speak.

As a final task, let me give you a taste of how I am presently using ROUTE to achieve mastery in another area; my writing. In that first speech, I had a decision to make at the point of fear. I felt uncertain and off-balance when I heard the news that I had to deliver the speech. The choices were clear. I could accept the challenge or sink back and remain comfortable.

The same was the case for my writing. First, I don't consider myself an exceptional writer. I am however better today than I was 10 years ago. Like public speaking, I remember being terrified to write. Writing was always a disjointed experience for me. I was always more comfortable talking ... if I had to choose between the two. I couldn't seem to capture my thoughts on paper. Today I recognize, as I did with public speaking, that I hadn't exercised my writing muscles. Just like in public speaking, I had to experience many of those early and uncomfortable moments to become better. I had to step out and risk comfort to advance my writing skills. You are now sharing in my writing journey.

So let me speak to the first action of ROUTE and the associated principle; it's the first and arguably the most important step in the process. That day as a sophomore in high school, I took a *Risk*, which is the first principle. The action that aligns with Risk is to Relish; I have discovered my need to Relish Risks. Meaning, I have to take pleasure in operating at the outer edge of my capability. I must delight in the chance to get out of my comfort zone. Until I take a risk, nothing's going to happen. Without risks, the process doesn't begin. There's a well-known expression "no risk, no reward." It's true! Many of us want the reward, but are not willing to take, and keep taking, the necessary risks.

Here's where this desire to write began. Several years ago I was experiencing some professional challenges with a boss. I remember trying to put my thoughts in writing. Maybe my emotions impeded the process; all I know is I couldn't finish the letter. There were a lot of words, but it said nothing. Have you ever been there! I got lost in my words. I was all over the place. There was no consistent message or path. I told myself "I *will* become a better writer." This statement itself was a risk, because now I had to do something about it. So I began the process of becoming a better writer.

The first step for me was simply to ratchet up my reading. I had heard that reading helped communication; not only verbal, but written. It did indeed enhance both my writing and verbal communication skills. To this day I have committed to reading a certain number of books each month; usually 2-3. Unlike some people, I don't always read different books within that month. I've discovered that it takes me longer to glean what I need from a book. So I usually read books 2 or 3 times before moving on; or I'll come back to them. So reading 24 books in a given year doesn't always mean 24 different books.

Amid this risk, here's an action that really helped my writing. This happened to be during heavy travel years. I had a blackberry phone with a notes application. I began to write every day. I would look for inspiration and write about it. It could have been a person I met, a difficult situation I was experiencing or something I had learned. Whatever popped into my head, I wrote about it. Over the course of 4 or 5 years, I accumulated hundreds of writings.

The point I want to make is this: My writing skills began to improve because I was doing it and doing it regularly. I began to feel more comfortable expressing myself in writing. My writing became more fluid; it felt a lot more natural. Again, I'm not the best writer. I can however get my point across when I need to; this writing is an example of that.

In the book, I talked about the 10,000 hour rule. I've read about this in *The Tipping Point* by Malcolm Gladwell and *The Talent Code* by Daniel Coyle. Both authors talk about these 10,000 hours as a prerequisite for achieving mastery in any area. Through my daily writing, I started to chip away at the 10,000 hours. I'm still on my journey toward achieving writing mastery.

There was another built-in benefit of this daily writing. It actually fed the content of the book. At a certain point along my daily writing journey, I got an idea about the structure for my book. Once I solidified that structure, I began to write about specific sections of the book. I began to look for inspiration and stories that aligned with the book structure. I was more targeted and intentional in my daily writing. As I wrote the book, I was able to refer back to and pull directly from these writings.

So here's the point: Just like speaking publically, I never thought I could write a book. I was embarrassed to allow people to read what I had written. It was tough. I was uncertain and unsure of myself. It was a risk for me to delve into a project like this. Again, at the point of fear, I had a choice. I could have remained in my comfort zone and not dealt with it or I could simply begin the process. I could have ignored my desire to write a book and not challenged myself in this area. I didn't. I stepped out of my comfort zone and took on the challenge of becoming a better writer. As a result of that decision, you are reading a portion of my writing today. Now my encouragement extends beyond what I do in public speaking.

There's an analogy that I use to describe how growth happens. I call it the cycle of education. It describes how we move through the academic process. From elementary school and beyond, it's how we ascend through the school system. Every time we transition to a different level, we must begin again. For example, when I transitioned from elementary to Jr. High (from 6th to 7th grade in my case) I had to drop to the bottom rung. In the 6th grade I was the big kid on the block. My next step was the 7th grade where I was, once again, an apprentice of sorts. I was humbled. My transition to high school from Jr. High school saw the same dynamic. From high school to college, the process was the same. After college, I was a management trainee. Some of you were graduate school students. And the cycle continues. Here's my point. There are times when we must fall to that bottom rung and begin the learning process over again; if we want to keep growing. Many times we forget this progression once we're out of formal education. And unfortunately, as a result, we stop growing.

I thought about this cycle when I decided to write a book. It was about becoming humble. The book was in line with my passion and purpose of encouraging and motivating, which fueled me incredibly. I first had to acknowledge the reality of where I was; the ugly truth about my starting point. This was my self-assessment. With an accurate self-assessment, I could do something about it.

This self-assessment can be risky business, because it's difficult to be honest with ourselves. I know I'm just as guilty as others; but it was hard for me to talk about areas where I wasn't strong. I wanted to focus only on strengths. Areas where I excelled! Arenas where I appeared to have things under control! I recognize some thought-leaders want us to focus purely on our strengths; and I believe there is a time for this. I've discovered however if I have a weakness but it aligns with my passion and purpose, I can develop that weakness into a towering strength. Public speaking was one of those areas; I've successfully transformed this weakness.

Going through the process of writing this book was at times painful. There was so much I didn't know. I had to learn. I had to ask people who had done it and then listen to what they had to say. I did that. I had to practice. I did that. I read a lot. I had no guarantee that it would work out; I had to trust the investment of time and the process. Would it someday turn into a book? This was the question. I can say today, I'm glad I started this journey. I'm glad I was honest at the outset. I'm thrilled I took the first step and saw the process through.

Today I am a better speaker and writer because I have learned to Relish Risks; healthy risks. I still have a ways to go in both arenas, but I will continue my improvement. As I grow older, my plan is to transition to even more writing. I was telling a friend the other day, I'm never retiring; and this writing skill that I'm now developing is the reason why. When I can no longer handle the rigor of speaking and facilitating, I'll still encourage through my writing. All because I abandoned comfort and gave writing a try.

Let me conclude with a few ways I am helping others overcome their fear of public speaking. In addition to writing this chapter and my upcoming book, there are a few things I am doing professionally and personally. First, I tell my story. I'm very honest about my journey and how tough it was for me. I don't want people to think I'm a natural. I'm not a prodigy. I want people to know the story; the full journey…the joy and the pain.

Second, as a part of my consulting practice, I lead presentation skills and communication workshops where I work with leaders on overcoming barriers and building skill. In these sessions, we practice a lot and I coach them. I'm always positive and I celebrate them a great deal. I use video…and we talk about ways to enhance effectiveness. I also provide one-on-one coaching to leaders. This is great, because we can focus exclusively on them and strategize about ways to bring their presentations to life.

Personally, I work with high school boys at my church. When I work with my boys, I actually have them lead some of our sessions. This is what one of my mentors did with me. I provide structure and coach them to embrace the early communication discomfort…and to trust the process of improvement. We talk a lot about mastery and how much practice it takes to get comfortable. I enjoy this because this is what I missed at their age. Being able to help others is truly the most rewarding part of the journey…and I'm always happy to do it.

Thank you so much for taking this short journey with me and I wish you the best in your journey. Look for the full book coming soon!

Reggie is often called dynamic. He's a coach-consultant with nearly 25 years' professional experience. Reggie is the founder of Lead Strong Inc., a Dallas based leadership consulting firm specializing in helping leaders and teams behave in successful ways. The 5 key behaviors are; connecting, communicating, collaborating, coaching and leverage conflict. He has traveled globally and worked with industry leaders like AT&T, BNSF, TCU, Lennox International, General Electric, Lockheed Martin, Honeywell, Texas Instruments, Marriott, Walgreen, BP, SAFRAN Group and others. An electrical engineer turned leadership enthusiast, Reggie is passionate about people and performance. He uses his business experience and his interpersonal effectiveness to help leaders and teams win…together.

**Reggie Carney**
Lead Strong
469-693-1552
Email: reggie@leadstronginc.com
Website: www.leadstronginc.com

Follow Reggie:
www.facebook.com/LeadStrongInc

# Becoming the Real You

## By John Carroll

*This chapter is dedicated to all of the shy introverts and under-achievers out there who struggle with self-limiting beliefs, and want to overcome them so they can move their lives in a positive new direction.*

During my childhood and early adult years, leader and leadership were words I would have never used to describe myself.

Growing up, I suffered from a lack of self-confidence and was very shy and introverted. As a result, self-expression, establishing new friendships and just basic communication with others was difficult for me. Moreover, I had a poor self-image and considered myself to be a classic under-achiever and a failure at many things that were important to me – i.e. sports, academics, personal relationships, etc. Consistently failing to "measure up" and falling short of my goals were not traits I considered to be reflective of leadership or leaders.

**My circumstances began to change, however, as a result of two life changing events and one simple sentence, "Do you know you don't look at people when you talk to them?"**

At the time, I was dealing with the trauma of the dissolution of my first marriage, a job loss and was at a low point in my life. All of my past self-defeating feelings of insecurity, inadequacy and personal failure hit me at the same time. However, rather than allowing these negative emotions to overwhelm me, I decided to take action and began to make some fundamental changes in order to move my life in a positive new direction.

What brought me to this turning point can be traced as far back as my early childhood. My parents were struggling financially, and as a result, we had to live in the upstairs of my grandparent's home in order for them to make ends meet. I remember sharing the limited upstairs area with another boarder. My grandparent's house did not have a furnace, so we would all gather around the space heaters with extra blankets to stay warm during the winter months.

When I was a little over four years old, my parents purchased their first home. It was a modest two bedroom house that we shared with my grandmother and great aunt. My bedroom was the sleeper sofa in the living room and we all shared a single bathroom, so it was crowded. My parents did their best to provide for our extended family. Both worked full-time until I was about 10 years old. We always had clothes to wear, albeit some were hand-me-downs from friends and neighbors, food to eat and a roof over our heads, but little left over for other things.

Even as a small child, I recognized life had not been kind to either my mother or father. Both of my parents came from broken homes and had to overcome enormous hardships and personal tragedies growing up during the Great Depression era. My mother was adopted and treated as little more than an indentured servant by her stepparents. She was forced to drop out of high school early in her sophomore year and worked long hours daily cooking, cleaning and doing odd jobs in the home and in her stepparents' general store to help support the family. My father's parents divorced before he finished high school. As a result, he had to live on his own and work on his father's milk route, delivering milk door-to-door, in order to support himself and complete high school.

**Looking back at my early childhood and my parents' financial struggles, it was as a small child that my self-esteem issues first began to surface. Inappropriately, I thought of myself as a second-class citizen because we were poor and lacked many of the material things that others families enjoyed.**

My parents had both been married previously, and they met and married late in life, after the conclusion of World War II. I was their only child together. My father had made it known on more than one occasion that he had wanted a girl. This fact stuck with me throughout my childhood and only served to diminish my self-esteem even more. My parents had a name picked out for a girl, but not a boy, so I became a "junior" by default. However, my father never referred to me by name, only "boy" or "Butch", a nickname written on my chart by a nurse at the hospital before my parents got around to picking out a name for me. Trust me; Butch is not a great nickname to live up to when you are the smallest kid in a neighborhood full of boys.

To say my father and I did not have a close relationship would be an understatement. He was a weekend alcoholic and was mean, loud and abusive when he had too much to drink. Reflecting on this period of my life has helped me understand why I began to display so much anger during my early childhood. My very first social interaction that I can remember came shortly after we moved into our first home. One of the neighbor boys greeted me with a rock to the back of my head. This was the first of several scars I received during those formative years.

There were six boys in our neighborhood, all about the same age, and two girls. So, we had numerous opportunities to get into fights during our testosterone filled adolescence. In fact, fighting became one of the defacto forms of communication back then. However, my fighting days pretty much ended during the sixth grade when I was expelled for two weeks after getting into a fight one day with the new kid in our class after a recess period. Try coming home from school and explaining that one to your parents.

On the weekends around our house it was like walking on eggshells because most of the time my father was a ticking time bomb. He was usually drunk and belligerent, barking out orders or snapping his fingers and calling me to do something. We never knew when he was going to go off, so it was difficult to have a conversation or to even approach him for that matter. Our family rarely got together, other than for Thanksgiving or Christmas dinner at our house, because of my dad's drinking.

From an early age, I felt like I was either adopted or from another planet because my goals and aspirations were so different from my parents and other family members. I never really had a family member that I felt comfortable going to for advice when I was struggling or just needed to talk with someone. As I grew older, I grew even more disconnected from my parents and family and we spent less and less time together and, for whatever reason, we were never able to find that common ground needed to just talk and enjoy each other's company.

From grade school to high school, I tried to go it on my own, and consequently went through a number of different phases in an effort to "come out of my shell" and get noticed by others. From the shy quiet introvert, to the talker, to the class clown, to the little tough guy, to the popular student-athlete and finally in high school, I just tried to blend in. Each of these phases was an effort on my part to gain recognition and acceptance from peers, teachers, coaches, etc. However, I really didn't do much to distinguish myself during any of these phases.

A recurring theme on my report cards was "John has a lot of potential, but needs to apply himself more in the classroom." This theme carried over into many other areas as well, including sports, extracurricular activities, social events, girlfriends, etc. However, I did become quite accomplished at one thing - giving up on myself when things got too tough and making excuses for my failures. Those of you who have been through similar experiences in your life know exactly what I'm talking about.

Next up was four years of undergraduate school and it is a blur today. Like most young people right out of high school, I didn't have a clue what I wanted to do with my life. In one of our rare father-son talks, my dad told me I should "go to college in order to make more money and stay out of Vietnam." Sounded reasonable to me, so I enrolled in college since all my friends were going, too. However, the best thing I can say about the college experience is that I survived. My parents were not able to provide any financial support, so my schedule from Monday through most Saturdays was consumed with work, homework and classroom studies and later on, outside activities with my first wife.

**The fondest memories of my four years of undergraduate studies were of spending time with friends, meeting my first love (she dumped me), meeting my first wife (we married after my sophomore year) and buying my first great car ... 1965 Ford Mustang (black).**

My first major shift toward the future occurred when I changed majors from accounting to marketing after my sophomore year. One of the reasons I enjoyed accounting so much was that I loved working with financial statements and figures. However, this was also the time I started listening to my inner voice that there were other things I should explore and be open to in order to expand my horizons. Had I known at the time that most Marketing majors were viewed as future salespeople to the outside world, I probably would have never changed majors. Being a salesman was the farthest thing from my mind at this point. My decision to change majors was based on pursuing a career in market research and new product development after graduation.

Why was a career in sales the absolute last thing on my mind? Because I thought of myself as a shy introvert with little self-confidence, and the idea of facing the public, making presentations and getting up in front of a large audience to give a speech was absolutely paralyzing to me. So much so that I had even postponed taking Speech class until I had to complete the course in order to graduate. I recall being the first person called upon to give a speech during the second week of class and the experience was absolutely horrifying. I was bright red, perspiring profusely and stuttering all the way through the speech.

What made it worse is that two of my classmates, Deanna Bowers (actress Dee Wallace) and Thelma Whitehead were both speech and oral interpretation champions. Knowing these two outstanding speakers were in the audience each time I had to present made the experience even more painful. During the first three or four years after college, I had two other opportunities to speak in front of large groups and, once again, both speaking engagements were horrifying to the point that I was fortunate to get through them without passing out.

In addition to launching my career after graduation from college, I also coached basketball at both the 6th grade and junior high level. The experience of working with young people helped me to grow tremendously, and enhance both my communication and leadership skills. My first managerial assignment came roughly 2 1/2 years after graduation from college. I was promoted to the manager of sales administration and support for a Kansas City-based manufacturing firm, with responsibility for Canada, Europe, all branches of the U.S. military abroad, the Middle East and Mexico. It was an uplifting, eye-opening experience for a kid from Kansas to be able to work within such a culturally rich environment and to learn from others about the nuances of leading people and business operations in highly diverse organizations.

During this same time period my first wife and I celebrated the birth of my oldest son. Up to this point my wife and I had had a rocky first few years of marriage. Her father committed suicide a little over two months after we were married and the family was never able to fully recover from the traumatic ending of his life. My wife took her father's death very hard. It strained our relationship to the point that we almost separated several times during the first two years of our marriage.

My next career assignment afforded me even greater opportunities for growth with another local manufacturing firm, where I took on broader responsibility for customer service and support for their U.S. and international sales operations. This was a more senior leadership assignment that required a major time commitment. Members of the management team were required to work a minimum of 10 to 12 hours a day, take work home in the evenings, and be in the office most Saturdays. This didn't leave a lot of time left over for family, and my wife and I soon began to drift apart. As my leadership responsibilities continued to expand, so did the hours and the stress. At the ripe old age of 26, I doubled up on the kitchen floor one morning with an ulcer. I was miserable both personally and professionally. My inner voice was growing louder, telling me it was time to make some much needed life changes.

From a maturity standpoint, I have heard that the light bulb does not generally go off for most guys until somewhere around 27 years old. For me, it was about three months before my 27th birthday. This is when I made the decision to ask my wife for a divorce and began to move my life in a new direction. I had now reached a new low point in my life. The realization I had failed as a husband and as a father to my young son was crushing.

What I did not anticipate, however, was that about 30 days after we separated and began filing the divorce papers, the company I worked for announced a major layoff and my position was eliminated.

Although my initial reaction of shock was soon replaced by a sense of relief, a job loss at this point was financially devastating. Between the divorce and the job loss, everything I had worked so hard for up to this point was gone – family, career, house, car, etc. Even more demoralizing was the fact that in order to regroup financially, I had to move back with my parents.

One night I remember breaking down as I sat on the end of the bed, feeling more disconnected from others than ever before. For the first time in a very long time, I began to pray and ask God for guidance to help me through this very dark, troubling period of despair. The next day I woke up more refreshed, with a renewed sense of focus and determination. After breakfast, I sat down at the kitchen table with pad and pencil and began to do my own self-assessment and life planning. Quite frankly, there were more minuses than pluses on the list, but I didn't beat myself up over it. Instead, I wanted to understand what got me to this point and where to go from here.

At this point, I wasn't ready to tackle the responsibilities of a sales position. However, I did enjoy working with people and wanted my next career assignment to be in public relations or a support role with daily contact to the general public. My prayers were answered when a position for a manager of provider relations with Blue Cross-Blue Shield of Kansas City became open. The job description was a perfect match with my goals, and afforded me the opportunity to work directly with the public in a non-selling role. Little did I know at the time that this career change would be a major turning point in my life.

After the initial series of interviews, I received and accepted the job offer and then began a 14-week training program. During the third week of training the director of provider relations, Bill East, called me into his office. He asked me to take a seat and told me he had a concern to discuss with me. Immediately, all of my fears and anxieties, self-confidence and self-esteem issues came rushing to the surface. My initial thought was "oh God here we go again, I'm going to get fired."

**Instead, Bill said "do you realize that you don't look at people when you talk to them?".**

I was absolutely stunned by his observation. Here I was almost 27 years old, been married for almost 7 years, have a child, own a home, and have had two prior international assignments and, in all this time, not a single person had ever brought this issue to my attention. Bill asked me to go home and practice in front of the mirror until I felt more comfortable, but just the fact that he brought this to my attention was enough. It helped explain a lot about my difficulties in the past relating to others. What I now began to notice was that people responded differently to me when I looked at them. And I began to build stronger, trust-based relationships as a result. This also helped me to overcome my shyness and self-confidence issues, particularly in group situations.

Although I haven't seen Bill in almost 30 years, I will always be grateful for his mentorship and support. Bill was the first person who took the time to work with me to overcome my self-limiting beliefs and become a better person. During our conversation, he also made me aware that we were getting ready to announce major revisions to Medicare and Blue Cross-Blue Shield reimbursement guidelines affecting hospitals, skilled nursing facilities and home health agencies. In order to communicate these changes to the provider community, we would be scheduling a series of seminars for large groups of hospital administrators and departmental personnel. Being a part of the provider relations organization meant that I would be one of the presenters at these half-day and full-day seminars.

In addition to working on my eye contact, I now had to face my biggest fear head-on, the fear of public speaking. This was no small task in view of my past failures in this area. However, I was determined to be successful in this new role, so the first thing I did to conquer my fear was to remind myself that "this is the path I've chosen, and if you don't do it you're going to get fired!" The idea of another job loss while I was going through a divorce was enough motivation to ensure I would not fail this time around.

The first thing I did was start making some basic changes in how I approached public speaking opportunities. For the first seminar session, I literally wrote out word-by-word exactly what I wanted to say during my one-hour presentation. Then I talked through it, edited it and went over it time and time again until I had memorized it verbatim. By the time the team met for a dry run, I was almost ready to go live. My presentation went off without a hitch (and I didn't pass out). Bill even remarked that I was so well prepared that I never looked back at charts during the entire presentation.

Working for an industry leader like Blue Cross-Blue Shield afforded me numerous public speaking opportunities, and a year later I received my first paid speaking engagement at a large symposium sponsored by the University of Kansas Medical Center. Being invited to speak at the conference was a huge boost to my self-image and validated how much progress I had made in overcoming my public speaking and self-confidence issues. For this particular three-day educational symposium, I was the only non-M.D. or PhD on the program. The feedback on my presentation was so positive that I was invited back to speak the next year.

As I gained more experience at public speaking, my self-confidence began to grow. One of the things I learned through this process that has helped me immensely in leadership roles is to learn to live with the 10% that doesn't go right. This holds true in preparing for a sales call, speaking engagement or any other situation in life for that matter. In the past, I was focused on perfection to a fault; if the phone call or presentation wasn't perfect in the first 30 seconds then it was a failure.

What I'm now able to do is to focus on the things that are within my control and not beat myself up when things aren't perfect.

Three years later, I moved into my first sales position with Blue Cross-Blue Shield as a national account sales executive. This assignment helped prepare me for what was to come over the course of a successful 30-year career in sales and marketing leadership assignments. Also while working full-time at Blue Cross-Blue Shield, I completed my Master of Business Administration (MBA) degree with distinction in 2.5 years from Central Missouri State University. Not too bad for a classic under-achiever who in the past "had shown a lot of potential in the classroom, but needed to apply himself".

In November of 1980, I left Blue Cross and Blue Shield and accepted a position as an account executive with AT&T. This career change proved to be another significant milestone in my personal and professional development. AT&T had just recently announced its national sales school and I was one of the people selected to participate in the pilot of the company's 9-month sales training program. After successfully completing the 9-month training program, I was assigned to my initial sales territory in Oklahoma City, and finished my direct sales career as an account executive at 275% of quota, in the top 5% of AT&T's national sales force.

During the past 30-years of my career, I have held Director, Vice President and COO positions with Fortune 1000, mid-size and emerging companies, and have led business divisions that generated more than $1 billion in revenue. In addition, I've received numerous sales, marketing and leadership awards, including being recognized by both Who's Who in Executives and Professionals and the Global Registry of Outstanding Professionals and Entrepreneurs for outstanding sales and leadership accomplishments.

Most importantly, I have been blessed with three outstanding adult children and three terrific grandchildren, and my second wife and I have been happily married for over 34 years. All of this from a shy introvert with little self-confidence who never envisioned himself being in a sales or a leadership position growing up. I wanted to share this chronology with you to illustrate what is possible when you start to believe in yourself, take charge of your life, get great advice along the way, and surround yourself with extraordinary people who will love you, lift you up and help you to succeed.

**"It's not how you start ... it's how you finish."**

And I'm far from being done! Today, I work with entrepreneurs and small business owners, from start-up to exit planning, to help them maximize business performance and achieve the results to move beyond their vision, both professionally and personally. Because of the diverse business and leadership experience gained throughout my career and as an elder in the church, I have had the opportunity to work with, coach and mentor hundreds of businesses and business leaders. These opportunities have included being a speaker at numerous sales kick-off meetings, seminars and training workshops and networking events.

**Here is what I have learned over the years that I hope will help you overcome the same or similar challenges in your life ...**

1. You don't get to pick your family, so find a way to love and support them despite their flaws. Remember, you have warts and liver spots, too!
2. If you're not uncomfortable, you're not growing. So, take on new opportunities and challenges outside your comfort zone and grow from them.

3. Life is not perfect, get over it. Apply the 10% rule to everything. Focus your energy on the 90% that does go right to build on those successes.
4. Learn to listen (and respond) to your inner voice of reason. Don't let the noise of others' opinions get in the way of your progress.
5. Failure is an integral part of life. Embrace it, learn and grow from it, but don't let it diminish you or keep you from achieving your goals.
6. Small things can have a major impact on a person's life. Take the time to reach out to and mentor others who could benefit from your wisdom.
7. Love yourself and get comfortable in your own skin. You'll be much better prepared to overcome any hardships or challenges ahead if you do.
8. You can't do it all without the help of others. Surround yourself with people who will love, support and encourage you to go higher. Avoid the energy vampires.

Throughout this chapter of the book, I have shared much of my own personal background with you. This was done not to showcase my life's challenges or accomplishments, but rather to emphasize that each one of us has the capacity to change, grow and accomplish great things despite our family history, personal disappointments or the obstacles that are placed in our path. Just believe in yourself, stay open to the possibilities, and take charge of your life by eliminating those self-limiting beliefs that are holding you back today.

Remember this always, God is more interested in changing us rather than our circumstances. He leaves it up to us to change our circumstances. So, if you are ready to take the next step and make positive changes in your life, then seek God's favor and guidance. Now get to work on becoming the person you were meant to be – **the real you**.

Enjoy the journey!

JOHN CARROLL is the founder and CEO of Tres Coaching Services™, a business and leadership coaching, consulting and training services company. He is also the author of Globalization: America's Leadership Challenge Ahead. In addition, he is a frequent speaker on sales, marketing and leadership topics included in his Back to Basics 2.0 ℠ business series. John works extensively with both entrepreneurs and small business owners to help them maximize business performance and "achieve the results to move beyond their vision."

John has three adult children and three grandchildren. He and his wife, Laura, live in Keller, Texas. For additional information please visit: trescoach.com or contact John directly at john@trescoach.com.

**John Carroll, Founder & CEO**
Tres Coaching Services™
Email: john@trescoach.com
Website: www.trescoach.com

Follow John:
www.facebook.com/trescoach
Twitter: @trescoach

# Following Your Passion Against All Odds

### By Maryellen Dabal

*I dedicate this chapter to all those individuals who have had passion for a goal and need inspiration to continue to reach that goal in spite of challenges. Life throws us many tests. Being able to accept the test, pass the test and achieve our goal in the end can be a most rewarding experience. You are worth the effort to achieve that goal, whatever it is, and benefit from the rewards it brings. Stay well.*

As I tell my story, I hope you will find hints of inspiration and excitement to take with you in your own life. While my story will not begin with childhood recollections, my challenges as an adult in pursuing a career with meaning and hope use the many lessons instilled in me as a child to overcome those challenges.

My story begins with learning that my family (husband and two daughters 2 and 5) will be relocating away from the only life we have ever known; a life filled with family birthday parties and gatherings with siblings, nieces and nephews and our parents. This is a choice my husband and I have made together and little did we know we would be making similar decisions several more times in our marriage.

We have now moved 700 miles away from family and I am settling into our new community where we know exactly one person in this state.....the person my husband borrowed a snow shovel from so we could dig out the driveway and back the moving truck up to the garage.

Ok now what? I have left behind a promising career with a major food company, along with all its benefits and traveled into the world of the unknown. Now don't get me wrong, we both love an adventure and have looked at this situation as an opportunity to experience something new. We also look at it as a way for my husband to advance his career in a way that is wonderful. We would not have moved if we both did not see the positives in it.

What has now become a pattern with us, and a tool I excitedly pass on to you, is that if you are making a decision with a loved one (husband, wife, significant other) whether you are purchasing a coffee table or moving to another country or anything in between, make that decision together. You are avoiding the possibility of it coming back to bite you later in the relationship. If you make the decision together then you either rise together or fall together, both knowing fully well what lies ahead to the best of your ability.

With a management/finance background I found myself in a place where I no longer had to work to provide for my family so I decided to go back to school. So how did I decide what to do? I actually sat down with the yellow pages and a list I had already created of what I wanted in my new career and what I felt were my strengths. I repeatedly paused at professions like "counselor" and "therapist" and "marriage counselor". I thought….that's what I want to do.

Through research I discovered LCSW (Licensed Clinical Social Work) programs, LPC (Licensed Professional Counselor) programs and LMFT (Licensed Marriage and Family Therapy) programs. I interviewed several individuals in various parts of the field and decided that, although it would be a harder road, that LMFT was the licensure for me.

I started graduate school at the University of Indiana, South Bend in 1999. There was no LMFT program per se but they offered a general counseling degree. I could transfer to an LMFT specific program later on down the road once I had done more research on what was available.

I juggled kids, a husband, living away from family and a desire to become more than what I already saw in the mirror. I was supported by my husband and two growing daughters at every turn. I would get a day to myself once in a while to work on papers, read extensively and just do what I needed to do. I couldn't have done it without all of them encouraging me along the way. One of my fondest Indiana memories was of my cat curling up on my lap in between me and my textbook on a cold winter afternoon when the girls were napping. He loved to read with me. He was the perfect fit for my lap and kept me company, too. Duncan, may you rest in peace. You were always a great study buddy.

I started out slowly with one class to get back into the swing of homework and learning to do papers, etc. again. I hadn't been in school for 13 years. And even then I didn't have a home to take care of, a husband and children. What was I doing? Could I handle all of this and still be happy?

My first class confirmed that I was in the right place. I was one of the oldest students in the classroom (30 something) but I also had a lot of life experience to offer that my fellow students couldn't even imagine. My most memorable class was one where we had to design a counseling center based on research we did in the community to find out how to fulfill a need. I still have the portfolio and would love to implement that someday.

***Wrench #1 thrown into the system:*** We had to relocate back to NJ for my husband's job.

I had worked very hard to put this new career path into action and was faced with a choice to make. I could be angry that I had to uproot again after only 3 years. I could be upset knowing I was only able to transfer a handful of my credits earned to another university due to regulations stating that a certain maximum experience from another state will be accepted. *(You will see as you read further that this fact will be a common theme in my journey.)* I could also accept that it was more beneficial for our family as a whole to relocate again and that, while it would take a little longer to get licensed, I was still moving forward. There was frustration for sure that I had lost some credits, but throughout this entire journey it was very important for my sanity to realize that no class and no client experience was ever a waste. All my experiences have contributed to my being even better at what I do every single day. It was a tough lesson to keep remembering as my quest continued, but it was truly necessary.

Now my family is settled yet again in another state, which happily surrounded us by family and I began my quest for licensure for the 2<sup>nd</sup> time. I interviewed with the head of the Marriage and Family department at Seton Hall University in August of 2001. I received the phone call in early September that I was accepted into the program and could start the following week, even though classes had started the week before. Something told me to wait until the next semester, in Jan, 2002, and to begin the semester with the rest of my classmates. I postponed my starting at Seton Hall until early 2002.

Little did I know that 9/11 would occur the following Tuesday morning, only a few days after my acceptance into the Seton Hall program. Having lost 11 people in our church and 26 people in our town, I was very happy that I chose to postpone my starting school and used that time to comfort those around me and refocus on what was important in life.

January, 2002......round 2 of schooling. New city, daughters a little older, I should be able to do this. Seton Hall actually had a program that specialized in marriage and family therapy, not just general counseling. I was very excited as this was more specific to what I wanted to do. The professors were amazing. My classes were challenging and they forced me to reflect and realize how lucky I was in life.

For example, during a class on creating Genograms (family diagrams) I volunteered to have my genogram drawn in front of the class. I soon realized that my background was one of support from my parents and siblings and I was encouraged to be whatever I wanted to be. I had no "family secrets", at least not that I knew of at the time. I did not have alcoholism or drug abuse as a family occurrence nor did we even have second or third marriages. My parents were married and have been married for over 50 years with no children from any other marriages. Having been in the industry for over 8 years now and having counseled many families along the way, I only now realize how truly unique that situation is. So much so that I even called my parents one day during that first semester to thank them for making life so "boring". I continue to value that aspect of my childhood years even to this day. My inspiration to continue and to look at life from a positive perspective has come from my parents and now also from the family my husband and I have created. I pray that some of that inspiration has been instilled in our daughters.

After going through that class and realizing how lucky I was to have been part of a family that was so "normal" it also meant that I might have a hard time relating to clients in challenging situations since I had not experienced much of that myself. So it became my goal to work in as many different environments as possible where I had no previous knowledge during my practicum and pre-licensure experiences.

While accumulating hours during my studies I initially worked at a traditional counseling center. I can remember the fear in my heart as I walked in to meet with my first client. Thinking back, I must have appeared so "raw" with my talent. I knew I had to dive in and give it my all and that's exactly what I did. Soon I was feeling more comfortable in the counseling room and began to seek out additional opportunities to fulfill my requirements for graduation. Knowing that I had continuous support from family, mentors and supervisors was crucial to staying on track and focused on the end goal of licensure and being able to attain as much knowledge along the way as possible.

I was offered a rare opportunity through a fellow graduate student to work in a correctional facility with adult males preparing to return to society. Could I help them and their families prepare for that release day? I was very hesitant to enter such an environment; with its metal detectors, its requirement to keep all personal information to myself and the fact that I was practically the only Caucasian on the property. It was an amazing 1 ½ years working in that environment in one of the most challenging cities; learning what it felt like to be a minority amongst the male population as well as the cultural population. Truly an eye-opening experience that to this day remains one of my most unique practicum sites and life experiences.

May 2005, Graduation Day. I was happy to have my family around me to celebrate this accomplishment. My daughters were coming to my graduation. How unique. I hope they were as proud of me as I was of myself that day. It took much diligence and self-determination to reach this day and I was going to absorb as much as possible to remember it. I hope I was able to show them that no matter your age, pursuing your goals and your passions was important at any stage of life.

I soon learned that I needed to switch to another correctional facility nearby to perform more of an assessment role with inmates just coming into the system. Afraid, but eager to experience even more of a diverse situation, I accepted the offer and once again had to learn the "ropes" of the new facility.

With that new facility came new challenges. I was no longer in a room with just one inmate and his family, but somewhere between 10 and 35 inmates who had just arrived and needed to be evaluated for current drug and alcohol addiction/abuse.

I didn't have to learn the ropes alone, though, as I had a very talented coworker to show me around and help me learn the protocol. Accompanying her to the assessment room was initially pretty terrifying but soon became the routine of walking down the hall and entering a cafeteria-sized room with a few dozen adult males waiting for direction from my coworker or myself.

Needless to say, while challenging and enlightening, I wondered where the tenacity came from to walk through those metal detectors every day and be able to focus on the job at hand. I had never been in a jail before, nor knew anyone who had ever been in that circumstance. How could I help these people? What knowledge would I have that could be given to them? I soon found out that the positive perspective that I grew up with was not something most of the inmates had ever experienced. Being respected as a person and being valued for what talents and gifts I helped them to find was something new for them. Most individuals in their lives either had taken them for granted or used them in some way. It was new for them to have someone just let them be themselves. I discovered what talents I possessed to share with them and used that to the fullest potential to influence as many of them as I could. I was put here for a reason. I now knew what that reason was.

From that facility I moved on to working in a high school setting whereby I observed and counseled teenagers with many different agendas. Some, who lived in foster homes, were thinking about all the chores they had to do when they got home. Some, who were pregnant, had to worry about getting to the doctor in time for a checkup. Still others were more carefree and had just the typical teenage issues of fitting in, or being the new kid or worried about an upcoming test. I helped them to take a moment to breathe, focus on what was most important right then and help them make a plan for a successful future.

***Wrench #2 thrown into the system:*** An opportunity to move to Texas with now a 5th grader and an 8th grader to enhance my husband's career. Yes or no? Well, of course it was a yes. We took a month to decide and, while I would have some licensure challenges moving to what is now home to us, we thought it was best to relocate. Again my husband and I sat down and discussed the pros and cons of our situation and decided together that it was the right thing to do. So we packed up our daughters and headed to the Lone Star State.

Prior to relocating and having not yet achieved full licensure, I contacted the licensing board in Texas to see what, if any, of my experience would count in Texas. Unfortunately the gentleman who told me that many of my experience hours would count was no longer employed at that facility once I physically arrived here. So here we go again....***Wrench #3*** or what I so thought.

I found a very experienced supervisor who introduced me to an array of talented professionals in the area. I researched various therapy association websites and engrained myself in as many groups as I could find. I began to establish a reputation for honesty and hard work that is finally beginning to pay off.

I was invited to be part of a local Association Board for Marriage and Family Therapy, which has allowed me to network with many area experts. I am grateful for their support over the years. I am also a part of our local newcomers club, which again, has allowed me to network with those that may be in need of my services at some time in the future. Networking is key to being successful in most professions but especially in this one. We cannot just post a picture and give a short bio and expect people to just "pick" us. While internet presence is proving to be very influential in the decision-making process, I truly believe that we must go out into the community in various ways and allow people to get to know who we are and what we stand for. I have found that those that trust me the fastest are the ones who were given my name as a referral from a trusted friend or those who have personally met me through some function in town and feel as though I know what I am talking about. I wear my compassion on my sleeve sometimes. That may be good or not so good but it is who I am and I embrace that every day of my life. Do we not ask our clients to embrace who they are, choose to change what they wish and live life to the fullest? I would be hypocritical if I did not do the same.

Having been in private practice now in Texas for almost 3 years, I checked back in with the licensing board to be sure I was on track with the hours needed for full licensure. Working in private practice was a slower road but due to my lack of connection to local MFT graduate school programs and my obligations to my family, it gave me the flexibility I needed to be able to be a wife and mom but also pursue my career on my own schedule.

Here comes *Wrench #4*.......

Well, to my surprise...*not*...I was told by the same representative that I have been working with ever since I relocated to Texas that still less of my hours would count towards licensure. Not sure where the consistency lies in the process but so far I have been able to roll with the punches, and there have been many. OK breathe.....we will work this out. I can continue to do what I am passionate about, but it will just take me a little bit longer to achieve that ultimate goal of full licensure.

Fast forward to the year 2011. I continue to work in private practice, network every waking minute, go to supervision, obtain a certification in a specialty as well as research yet another specialty, using my limited funds after rent, phone, advertising, etc. I am moving forward.

OK, according to my records, with my reduced amount of hours accepted from my last place of residence, along with the hours I have acquired in Texas, I am one month away from full licensure. I can taste the license. I can smell the initials changing from LMFTA to LMFT.

One more call to the licensing board to be sure I am on track for licensure and I am told that after further review NONE of my hours from my last state will count. Yes there was steam coming out of my ears. I was furious. The individual I have been dealing with for over 3 years, who continued to differ in her opinion as to which hours would be accepted; who would never put anything in writing is disappointing me for yet another time. I was always pleasant on the phone. I always sent confirmation letters after our conversation, thinking, heck, if she wasn't going to put anything in writing, at least I was.

November, 2011. I pulled out the carton containing all of my licensure information from various states (DO NOT EVER THROW ANYTHING AWAY!!!). I pulled out what I needed from my previous state, and sent the information needed to make an unusual request. Would they please review the forms I have sent and confirm that I in fact had worked the hours listed post-graduate and to please inform the Texas Licensing Board that I had done so. Now I sit and wait for them to meet in 2 weeks. But will they agree with my findings? Will they finally give me what I have worked for since 1999?

Good news. They graciously accepted my information, provided proof to the Texas Board of my accomplishments and forwarded this proof as requested. This was still not enough for full licensure though. But I was not far away. Whewwww.

Finding cooperation throughout this process has not been easy. I respect the Board's function in protecting the public from unqualified individuals receiving licensure but I would still support a country-wide continuity of requirements as relocating throughout this wonderful country is becoming much more of a habit for many in my field. From my experience, most professionals in this field have a passion for helping others and a true desire to make a difference. I only wish those at the Licensing Board offices could feel that passion as well. That's not something that can be shared on an application. Perhaps a video of why we are seeking this licensure should be submitted with the paperwork.

As I reflect back on the journey so far, I have seen obstacles be overtaken by a desire to reach a goal. I have seen disappointments turn into triumphs due to the perseverance of my soul and my family to help me achieve something so important in my life. While the letters after my name reflect an individual status, the dedication and meaning behind it belong to my family, my professors, my supervisors and the many individuals who have helped me along the way.

Early January, 2012. I am now preparing my final documents to be sent to the Texas Licensing Board with the utmost care and precision. I am double and triple checking each document to be sure the numbers are correct, the fees are correct, and nothing is missing. I nervously secure all my documents in a sealed 2" thick letter size box and put the proper address on the front. I proceed to the post office with the last 13 years of my life's work inside. Will it get there? I take every precaution to be sure it is signed for on the other side and I get a name of who has my documentation. I nervously wait….and wait….and wait.

After about 2 weeks I still have not received a call. I contact the board and talk to the woman I have been dealing with for 4 years now. She has my packet of information and has some questions. I answer the questions and with my heart pounding, await a response. She informs me she has to add some figures together and review a certain portion before she can give me an answer. I am about to welcome my next client into my office and cannot stay on hold. She tells me she promises to call back as soon as she has my answer. I have no choice but to agree and hang up.

My phone sits beside me as I speak with this client. I see it light up with the words Texas Board as the identifier. I begin to sweat. I finish my session with my client, escort them to the door and walk back to my office. I take a deep breath. Should I wait until I get home to check the message? No way. I could not contain myself and dialed into voicemail. Good news was delivered and I have been approved for full licensure. I had to replay the message three times before it sank in. My certificate of proof would be printed tomorrow and would be in my hands by the end of the week.

I stood there in awe. I had done it. I had reached the goal of my profession and the goal I had set for myself 13 years ago. I teared up just a little. I smiled. I was proud of myself in that moment for enduring all the ups and downs that brought me to this place. I was thankful for all those who supported me along the way. I hugged myself and sat in silence for a few moments just to take it all in.

I saved that message on my phone for 4 months before finally deleting it. I received my certificate as planned and was able to move on with other goals for my career, including being incorporated and seeking other certifications only available to me after having achieved full licensure.

I have been fully licensed for 7 months now and I am thankful every day for what I endured in order to be able to enjoy that one moment of listening to that voicemail. If we don't endure hardships in life, it is difficult to appreciate the good times and the moments of reaching the goal you have set. I wouldn't change any part of my journey. I am thankful for having reminded myself to continue to move forward. Now, don't get me wrong, I had several times of questioning whether or not to continue over the years, but through it all I was always reminded that this was my passion and whatever I had to endure, *it* was worth the effort because *I* was worth the effort.

I dedicate my life's work in this field to my very first supervisor, Paula Fitzsimmons, LMFT, who helped me sort through all the challenges, define how to overcome them and was there to celebrate many of them with me as well. Unfortunately I am unable to tell her that I have reached the end of the licensure journey. She passed away in 2010 but I know she is watching me from above. Her tassels from her own graduate school ceremony hang in my home office as a constant reminder that perseverance will pay off.....eventually.

I hope my journey to licensure inspires you to pursue your life's passion. I have enjoyed putting this journey on paper and sharing it with those who choose to read it. Know that you are worth the effort in anything you pursue. Surround yourself with those that inspire you and those that look at the positive perspective of life sometimes when you are unable to do so. I wish you all the happiness that life has to offer. Embrace it.

Stay well.........

Maryellen Dabal works with individuals, couples and families Monday through Friday from 8am til 8pm as well as select Saturday mornings throughout the month helping her clients to find the inner strength to be their best.

Her therapeutic philosophy is a combination of believing that discussions of the past can help you to understand where you have come from, which allows you to be able to define where you are today, which further aids in the creating of goals needed to help you reach your full potential.

Her role as therapist is to assist you in the transitions and issues that have you challenged with YOU AS THE EXPERT IN YOUR LIFE.

She holds a Post-Master's degree in Marriage and Family Therapy and a Master's degree in Applied Psychology, both received from Seton Hall University in 2005.

She has been in private practice in Southlake since 2008 and specializes in helping couples through the Marriage Life Cycle. She is certified in the Prepare/Enrich Marriage preparation program for those preparing to start that rewarding journey. She helps individuals, couples and families focus on a positive perspective to solutions and challenges as they experience the wonders of marriage. Should the marriage need to end for any reason, she is most recently trained as a Communications Facilitator for the collaborative law process that aids couples in achieving divorce without turning over total control of their assets and the process to the courts.

Add to that her experience of being married for over 20 years, having raised two wonderful daughters and having moved around the country, she believes that she has some quality firsthand knowledge of life experience to add to those degrees mentioned above.

**Maryellen Dabal, MA, LMFT**
Southlake Counseling & Neurofeedback Center
420 N Carroll Ave, Suite 140
Southlake, TX 76092
817-876-9958
Email: Maryellen@dabalmft.com
Website: www.dabalmft.com

Follow Maryellen:
www.facebook.com/pages/Maryellen-Dabal-at-Southlake-Counseling-NC/299454466770591

# Overcoming the Shadows

### By Nansii Downer

*It is my sincere hope and prayer that my words will encourage you to look beyond the darkness of where you once lived and step up and then step out. Feel the soothing warmth of the sun shine on your face. Breathe in the clean air of courage. Listen to the whisper of the wind as it calls your name with pride. Smell the sweetness of the honeysuckle that grows in your own backyard. Experience life. YOUR life. And then share the joy of putting your fears aside with someone else. You be their light, just like my friend was for me.*

*This chapter is dedicated to my many 'brothers' and 'sisters' who, like myself, have had to overcome the shadows. Think of that time in your life as a journey, a sojourn. You were never meant to stay there. It was only a stop along the way to get you here. And let me be the first to welcome you!*

I have never really been the kind of person that wants to be in the limelight. I enjoy doing things behind the scenes so as not to bring undue attention to myself. If the people in charge didn't know my name, well, that was okay with me. The ability to just blend in with the crowd was a trick I learned very early in life. If you didn't see me, then you couldn't get angry with me. Yes, blending in was a talent that I honed the skills of for much of my life.

If you were raised in a dysfunctional family, like I was, then I am sure that you can understand this mindset. Growing up in the 50's and 60's a common description for the perfect home was "Children are to be seen and not heard." Anyone remember that or am I really dating myself here? It was much safer to be "unseen" and "unheard" in my home. There was a precarious balance that was monitored all the time. There was also a lot of alcohol that was consumed most of the time. So the amount of "un"-happy juice consumed by the four adults (parents and grandparents) dictated the type of atmosphere in which my older sister and I tip-toed through each evening.

The thing about alcohol abuse is this; it will destroy anything and anyone in its way. It has no loyalty. It has no heart. It doesn't care that it breaks families apart. It blinds a grownup to the fact that they shouldn't drive. It makes them yell and hit you just because you happen to be home. An empty bottle in the trash only means that there is a fresh one in the pantry. From a child's view, me as a child anyway, the abuse of alcohol was the reason that everything in my home was a mess.

It's a long story of heartache and sorrow, but needless to say, I didn't have many words of encouragement or moments when these people were glad that I shared a life with them. I know that this statement must seem harsh, but I knew in my heart that I was the cause of my mother's daily drinking and her cancer. Why did I know this? Because she told me. Over and over again. My mother, in her illness, because only now am I truly able to comprehend how ill she really was, thought that her pregnancy with me was what gave her the ovarian cancer that eventually took her life almost 20 years later. She was diagnosed when I was 13 and she died the day before I turned 20. It was an extremely long and heartbreaking 7 years of being responsible for her illness. I never understood how I could've fixed it for her; I just knew that her drinking, her suicide attempts and her eventual death were because she got pregnant with me.

As a young adult, I didn't really know *who* I was, just who I didn't want to be. I didn't want to be like *them*. I wanted to be different. I wanted to love and be loved but I didn't know how. I was molested by my grandmother so I had a fear of trusting people. Most survivors understand this fear. Because my abuser had been a woman, and the fact that my mother usually drank on a daily basis for as long as I can remember—and shared with me how much she truly despised me and blamed me for her illness—I didn't know how to be a mother. It didn't come naturally to me because deep, deep, deep in my heart and mind, mothers hurt their children; emotionally and physically. So I kept everyone at arm's length. Even my children. Now don't get me wrong here. I loved my children then and I love them all now. But I have a deeper more secure feeling now of what love is, so I am able to cherish my children in my heart in a way that I had never known myself. Why? Because I overcame the shadows.

When my husband Bryan and I moved here to Texas, I thought that things would be different. I thought that I could forget the past that was somehow driving me and start fresh. A clean slate so to speak. No one would know me so no one could judge me. But as with most wounded warriors, I brought all of that baggage with me in a big ol' suitcase and promptly unpacked it. And as is with most abuse survivors, I didn't even see myself doing it. My pattern of running from people and avoiding relationships was more natural to me than my naturally curly hair.

And then I met Paula. I don't have to tell you her last name. She knows who she is. But more importantly the Lord knows who she is and how she allowed Him to work through her to help me. As Bryan and I walked into a new church one Sunday morning, we were greeted by Paula who smiled and welcomed us (I think she could tell we were new to the church) and then did the most unthinkable thing. She gave me a bear hug!! I almost fell over from fear. This woman, this happier than should be humanly possible WOMAN hugged me. My first thought was that I would NOT be going back to that touchy feely church again. But guess what? My husband felt compelled that we return there. And so we did. Week after week. Sunday after Sunday. There were other doors that we could chose, but oh no, each Sunday we found ourselves at Paula's door, her outstretched arms just waiting to hug me.

After about 2 months of visiting the church and being greeted by Paula each Sunday morning, she announced to me that the Lord had told her that He wanted me to be a greeter with her. My first reaction was that we of course MUST be serving a different God, because the One that I served most assuredly would NEVER tell her to tell me that. I smiled sweetly and declined her offer. The very next week she told me this same piece of news. The Lord wanted me to do this. I told her again that she must be misunderstanding the Lord. I didn't want to go into great detail of my fear of people with this stranger but at the same time I needed her to understand that what she was asking me to do was just…well, impossible.

Paula was persistent and called me on the phone to speak about me being a greeter. Paula said she understood my fear and apprehension, but more importantly she had faith that the Lord would not ask me to do something if He wasn't going to take care of me. In other words, no one would hurt me if I stood at the door and greeted them on Sunday morning. He would protect me. I couldn't for the life of me figure out why in the world the Lord would even want a person like me to be doing something so important in His church. Don't you see, I *knew* how bad I was. Shouldn't the Lord have known that and steered clear of me? Why would He want someone like me at the front door of His church?

There's an amazing thing about God and the plans He has for us. Because of my childhood experience I didn't have a very good relationship with the Lord. I didn't really trust Him nor did I think that He cared about me. I told Paula that I would pray about the issue of being a greeter and let her know. I wanted to just flat out say no. I wanted to, I tell you, I really did. But for some reason I kept feeling this tug in my heart and mind that I really needed to say yes. Crazy huh? I was a greeter at that church for about 3 years, for all 3 services. Very few people knew this at the time, but I was so frightened of people, that I used to get physically sick in between the services. Sometimes on Sunday morning I would plead with my husband to let me stay home, and most times he would simply say "Get in the car dear, you will be fine." He believed, like Paula did, that the Lord would never ask me to do what He wouldn't equip me for. I am glad that they trusted the faithfulness of the Lord for me when I couldn't do it myself.

My trust level towards people began to grow when Bryan and I started our cleaning company. I not only had to talk to people on the phone to set up appointments, but then I had to go and do the estimates. At first I thought "No way," but as time went by and my trust of the Lord got greater, so did my trust of others. Forcing myself to make those cold calls and then go and walk the house and give the customer an estimate changed me for the better. I grew. I became confident in what I did and what I said. Even on occasions when Bryan didn't go with me to do the initial estimate, I became calmer and calmer. I put my trust in the Lord and held on tightly. In 2012 we celebrated 14 years of service to our clients.

Almost 7 years ago we joined forces with *The Cleaning For A Reason Foundation*. We are a local chapter for them here in Tarrant County. When women are undergoing cancer treatments, our company goes and cleans their homes for free once a month for four months. I lost my older sister to breast cancer as well as my grandmother, and my mother

123

died of uterine cancer. To be able to do this small thing for these women is an honor for us. I told someone once that we can't make the cancer go away, and we can't make the fear go away, but we can come and clean their home. As women, if we can keep our home in a semblance of order, we can handle anything that is thrown at us. But, if the house is in disarray, everything becomes overwhelming. Women need to have a clean and orderly home while they are battling this disease so they can focus on getting well.

As our company grew we became more and more active in the community. Or at least my husband did. He attended chamber of commerce meetings, luncheons and other community events, to the point of eventually serving on the Board of Directors for the NETC Chamber. I wanted to stay home. I lacked the confidence that was needed to "meet and greet." To boldly go where no man has gone before was not my idea of the perfect night out. To network with others meant, well, that they got to know you and that wasn't a picnic that I wanted to share a blanket at. But for those of you that have met my husband, you know he can be a bit persistent. Especially if he thinks it is something that I *should* do. Like be with him at these events. I can remember many a time standing almost behind him in the hope that others wouldn't notice me. And believe it or not, I thought that the people in these groups were only nice to me because I was married to him and they liked him so much. I was liked out of default.

It was because of my relationships through these groups that I learned the importance of bringing your time, talents and treasures to others. I volunteered at a fundraiser and was hooked. By giving of myself to someone else a need was met in my soul. It is hard to describe the immense satisfaction I feel when I work with others for a common goal: helping someone who needs us. At the end of the day you are plum tuckered out in the best way possible. When you hear a soft yet heartfelt "thank you" it almost takes your breath away. Because I truly believe that this is a "God thing," I don't experience the "people fear" like I used to.

And it was here, through my volunteering for others that I changed, and I changed for the much better. For some reason I was able to convince others to help me on these volunteer events. For some reason, because I was able to do this, people then saw me as a leader. An organized volunteer machine that, when asked, could rally the troops to get a job done well and joyfully to boot. By taking the focus off of me and putting it where it belonged, on someone else's needs, I gained the confidence I needed to be successful at just being myself!! And my rewards have been wonderful. I served on the Board of Directors for the Northeast Chamber of Commerce for 5 years and on the ArtsCouncil Northeast for the last 3 years. Me!!

For the last 2 years I have had the privilege to work for a non-profit agency that brings meals and a whole lot of hope and joy to the shut-ins in my area. For me, it is a perfect job. In my position, I oversee the isolated seniors in the area and bring to them volunteers that can visit or call them on a regular basis. We also lend a hand when we can by doing odd jobs for them or running errands. You know, the kind of things that most of us take for granted but that they can't do any longer. Sometimes just knowing that someone is going to call or stop by is the only reason that a senior needs to get up and get going in the morning. I can't say this enough, "If you don't have a reason to get out of your jammies in the morning, you won't." The seniors that I work with need that reason. They can live a healthier longer life because of the kindness of others.

If there is one thing that I know for sure about all of us, if we live long enough, we will indeed need the love, care and support of others to help us through our days. I go from place to place within Tarrant County and help others to learn how to be a good neighbor so that they can take care of their neighborhood. It is the strength and unity of our neighborhoods that will keep us living good healthy long lives. We have to understand and accept that we need each other and then be willing to help each other.

When it is all said and done at the end of my day I think that I am the epitome of that old saying "You've come a long way baby." From brokenness to fruitfulness. From pessimist to optimist. From fear and sorrow to overflowing joy. From unresolved issues to a redemption by faith. I look around now and expectantly wait for the Lord to lead me. When I look in the mirror I don't see a scared child in an adult body any longer. It has been permanently replaced by a woman filled with the love and light of the One who has called her to serve Him.

I used to feel like I lived under this shadow of darkness and gloom. A lifelong sadness filled my heart and soul. I tried to hide who I was so that others wouldn't know how bad I was. I have now come to understand and be grateful for that time in my life. Oh no, don't think that I am grateful for the hateful words and child abuse because I am not. I am grateful though to my Savior who continued day after day and year after year to whisper His loving words into my heart waiting, waiting, waiting for me to believe and accept. It is because of His love, because of His power to overcome in me what I couldn't do alone, that I was able to forgive it and forgive it all. No more am I a victim, I am more than a conqueror because of my Savior.

At some point in time, the right time I believe, we have to stop punishing ourselves for our past mistakes, failures and pain. We just have to. My days used to be filled with such sorrow over the loss that I felt. It was overwhelming and consuming. Please notice that I said "was." You can change your mind and you can change the way you feel about yourself and the world around you. I am living, breathing proof of that.

A few years ago Bryan and I attended a small church that had a seminary with it. I offered to help out in the office and they generously offered to take care of any classes that Bryan wanted to take. Sweet huh? Well, here is something sweeter. They offered me a scholarship for classes for the entire 5 years I worked there. Isn't it amazing how the Lord works and prepares you to do the things that He has for you? Those years at the seminary gave me a wealth of knowledge and a love for studying God's word!! I will always be grateful to them (Thanks TTS).

About 4 years ago Bryan was asked to come up to a church in Argyle and teach their Wednesday Bible study group. It was a small group of mature believers who enjoyed sharing the word and fellowshipping together. We eventually pledged our membership there so that I would feel plugged in while we were busy planting a church in our own town. I had the privilege of being asked to lead the ladies Sunday morning Bible study. Because the Sunday Bible study classes don't meet during the summer, the ladies and I decided to continue the study via email. Our small group of about four women started with our first book. I would email my thoughts to them and they would send their thoughts back to me. We did this the entire summer. When we were almost finished, one of the ladies saw me on Facebook and sent me a message joking that I should be writing our study instead of playing on Facebook. One of my friends saw that post and asked if she could join our study. Then another and another. Would you believe that not only my friends and even friends of friends follow this email Bible study, but there are people that I don't even know that also follow it!! It now goes out to over 150 individuals in 12 different countries who then forward it on to people I may never even meet.

Each time I write one of my daily devotionals or on-line Bible studies, it is done through the power of the Lord who has given me the faith and the ability to do what He needs me to do while I am here on earth. My heartfelt desire is to be able to reach someone, who like I was, needs to hear the redemptive message of His love and grace; a message that can and will change their future. Their future here and their eternal future too.

"For you were bought with a price; therefore glorify God in your body and in your spirit, which are God's." 1Cor. 6:20

I have published "The Redemption of Ruth' from one of the email studies, and the next one "A Queen's Ransom: The Story of Esther" is almost ready for print. I even wrote and published a book of funny short stories called "Better Late than Never." And now this, writing my chapter in this book with others who just like me went out on a limb and tried to do what seemed impossible to them!! Learn to overcome the shadows.

Life is truly unbelievably amazing. We may not all have had a cookie cutter happy go lucky childhood. You may find that your soul is troubled and your heart is weary. But look around you. There are all kinds of folks, just like you, that need to get to know you so that they can get to know themselves. They need to hear your story. They need to sit a spell with you and hear how you put the past behind you and moved onward toward the blessing. Life has so much more to offer than you can ever imagine. Just step up and step out. You can do it. I know you can.

When you least expect it, life will offer you something that will truly bless you. For me it was the opportunity to bless others.

Nansii Downer has a heart as big as Texas and a spirit to help and encourage others in ways that never cease to amaze. She is an advocate for the marginalized and a strong proponent of social justice.

Her passion is to reach out to others with the love of Jesus and help them to realize their true potential in life.

Nansii is a mother of three great kids and a grandmother of the three greatest grandkids in the world. She lives in North Texas with her husband Bryan, their two dogs, Shady and Heidi and their faithful cat, Barney.

By day she works for a local non-profit helping to meet the needs of the area's isolated senior citizens. By night she enjoys cooking and hanging out with some of the best people in the world. She also helps her husband in ministry at Home Town Community Church.

She is an avid writer and has published two books. Her third book will be released soon. She loves to share the joys of the journey of life and seeks to lift others to heights they could not have imagined for themselves.

**Nansii Downer**
Email: Nansii@NansiiDowner.com
Website: www.NansiiDowner.com

Follow Nansii:
www.facebook.com/nansii.downer.author
Twitter: @NansiiD

# The Whisper and the Teachers

By Jim Gardner

*The following chronicle is dedicated to Louis Bourlard, my two children, Calais and Griffin who rock my world, and to all of the ageless children in this world who could use a little hope and inspiration.*

I was living what I thought was a normal childhood. That is until my 5<sup>th</sup> grade year when my mom threw my dad out for her infatuation with an escaped convict.

Over the next eight years I was screaming down my highway to Hell, committing virtually every crime you can imagine, and all but flunking out of school. Then I was stopped, almost cold in my tracks about halfway through my senior year in high school by my government teacher.

The following story is my own and I write these words to provide hope for those in the darkness and as inspiration for others who are looking for visions that will become their legacies. Names have been changed and omitted to protect the innocent and the guilty.

By the time I was 13, I fell asleep most nights petrified, with my hands on the steel bar and knife hidden under my mattress on the floor of my 8 foot by 8 foot room. You see, I never knew what was about to happen. Would it be drunken card games? Who would get shot, stabbed or beaten? I never knew what to expect.

I hated school because I was a poor reader. I couldn't concentrate. When I had homework, it seemed to take forever to complete. I struggled to understand the instructions for many of my assignments. I skidded by with C's and D's. By that time my dad had remarried and moved out of state.

All I knew was that I wanted to escape the Hell that had become my life. I would pray to God to take me away. I often thought of ways to end my own life, but I never could pull the trigger. I dreamt of how to cast away to another country where no one would know me and no one who had would ever be able to find me. I just never could come up with the foolproof plan.

My best friend Rick lived across the street from me as he had since we had moved in just before I started 1$^{st}$ grade. He was also in 5th grade when one evening he came running out of his house, screaming for help. His mother had just attacked his dad with a butcher knife.

My maternal grandparents owned a very small trailer park that had belonged to my grandpa's parents. There were hookups for maybe 12 trailers in the whole park. Weston Parker had recently moved his family into my grandparent's tiny mobile home park.

My grandparents invited the Parkers to one of our family get-togethers at their house. As it turned out, Mr. and Mrs. Parker weren't married after all and the young girl with them was not Mr. Parker's daughter. It was all a front to try to hide the fact that Wes Parker was an escaped convict from North Carolina. It was like a prequel to the movie *Cool Hand Luke*. Wes Parker had scars all over his body from working on chain gangs and from multiple stabbings and gunshot wounds.

Wes turned himself in to the authorities and served out a few short months in prison. Once he was out, he was spending more and more time at my mom's house.

It was the late 60's. There was the Summer of Love in San Francisco and Woodstock in New York. Sandwiched in the middle was Wichita Kansas, boiling over with racial strife. Black kids being bussed into schools, citywide curfews, car bombings, and law enforcement snipers consumed the local news. Race and color differences had no meaning for us in elementary school, but almost overnight it had become a point of significance in junior high. There was constant tension in the air and kids hung out in groups based on socioeconomic status and by color. I didn't feel like I really belonged anywhere.

My grandparents and an aunt and uncle were bright spots in my otherwise dark world that was beginning to spiral into the abyss.

My life on the streets was becoming darker and darker. What had been mostly mischief was turning more violent. Although I had a newspaper route, I was stealing for money. Drugs and alcohol were entering my scene.

Sometime during my ninth grade year, Wes Parker died of a heart attack underneath a house where he was repairing the plumbing.

Mom didn't waste much time finding the next stellar citizen to bring into our lives. Durwood Green was a lifelong Skid Row alcoholic. At the time he was sober, but that didn't last long. Durwood actually married my mom, something she was never able to convince Wes to do. Soon thereafter Durwood was literally never seen or heard from again.

As a sophomore in high school, I continued to fall further behind academically. I became the most truant kid in the second largest high school in the state. With about two months of the school year remaining, I was informed by school administrators that I was flunking every class and had skipped almost 200 hours of class time.

**The Whisper:**  As much as I disliked school, I heard The Whisper. "You ultimately have to graduate."  I met with all of my teachers to find out what, if anything, I could do to salvage a passing grade. I became totally focused for two months, and with tutoring help from teachers and friends, I passed all of my classes with C's and D's.

My best friend Rick and I were pretty decent basketball players.  On Sunday mornings, we were often invited by our black brothers to one of the gyms on the university campus to play pickup ball with some of the local college and pro athletes that showed up.

On Friday nights, some of the same brothers would sneak Rick and me to a YMCA deep in the heart of the ghetto to play ball.  We were the only white boys within five miles of the place.  The "Y" was always packed to the rafters with spectators.  If you were a gamer, you were a hero.  The games usually went on until 1:00 or 2:00 AM when we would be snuck back out to the more diverse world.

**The Whisper:** I heard The Whisper. "Be a leader.  You have to work harder to develop trust and respect since you are the different one and out of your element." Especially as an outsider, I had to restrain myself. There were hard fouls and differences of opinion on rule infractions. A wrong gesture or comment could have resulted in significant bodily harm.

One early morning after leaving the YMCA about 2:00 AM, several of us agreed to stop down the street at a chicken shack for some food.  I'm not talking about KFC or Popeye's, this was a real chicken shack.  Rick and I were sandwiched between several brothers.  As we entered the door, I noticed the man at the register had his right hand under the counter.  He hollered out.  "Ain't servin' no white!"  The next picture I expected to see was down the barrel of the gun he was holding under the counter, Rick fired back.  "I was gonna order thighs…"  Instead of

134

the crack of gun fire, I was stunned to hear laughter from the man behind the counter. He said "You boys is cool, come on in."

At 16, I got a job working in the produce department of a grocery store. Although I now had a part-time job, my unlawful habits continued. In some cases it was for additional income, but more often than not it was for the thrill of the chase. For quick money, public newspaper dispensers were an easy mark. The dispensers were usually chained down in the vicinity of the entrance to retail establishments. Dimly lit parking lots provided enough cover to pull up next to a dispenser, cut the security chain with bolt cutters, load the dispenser in the van, and exit the parking lot all in less than 15 seconds. Then it was simply a matter of prying open or blowing open the coin box. Local rivers were the grave yards for the then useless dispensers.

Everyone wanted 8 track tape players and car stereos no matter where they came from. Full service gas stations and used car lots were fertile grounds to lift these gadgets. It was amazing how often vehicles were left unlocked overnight in these parking lots. If a vehicle was locked and the risk factor seemed low, we made our own explosive devices to shatter the driver side window for easy access to the electronic goods. If noise was a risk, a slim-jim was a handy tool to unlock vehicles. Once we sold our haul, we then had the funds to purchase mind altering consumables, food, music, gasoline, etc.

Rick got a job at the theater as a doorman. He made friends with the theater manager, Anthony. So, when the next doorman position opened, it was easily mine. The motorcycle racing movie *On Any Sunday*, played for several weeks. John Boon, who owned a local motorcycle shop, and Anthony worked out a deal to display 3 motocross race bikes in the theater lobby. Rick and I were often left to close down the theater after the late show. After we had everything shut down, we would take the bikes into the theater and coast race them down the two slopped isles. I was hooked on motocross. I quickly learned motorsports were expensive, so I had to up my funding game. As it turned out, Anthony was the biggest thief I had ever met. He introduced Rick and I to stealing big ticket items like high end home stereo systems and TVs. Unknowingly we had crossed the line into grand theft.

My love affair with motocross gave me career aspirations of becoming a professional. Motocross is a grueling physical sport, so I began running 3 to 5 miles religiously every night at 9:00 PM. I figured I could continue racing and after graduation, go to work for a motorcycle shop selling and fixing bikes.

**The Whisper:** I heard The Whisper. "If you're going to compete at motocross, you must develop yourself." I had to practice riding and train my body. I had to hold myself to a schedule if I wanted to be any good.

Nothing much changed during my senior year except for a new job working in an independent grocery store, Vernon's. This time Bill, the owner, put me to work in the meat market. After about six months, in addition to continuing to cut meat on Saturdays, Bill gave me the responsibility of managing the baking isle. I had to stock and face the aisle every afternoon when I reported for duty. I then had to place the inventory orders for the items in my aisle.

The store was across the street from a junior high school. Every afternoon when school let out, the store was flooded with kids, several of whom, would steal candy and gum. Bill knew what was going on, but he couldn't figure out how to stop the problem. It takes a thief... I suggested to Bill that if he would install 2 way mirrored glass on the back wall at the end of the candy aisle, I could stand on a ladder in the stock room and catch the little thieves. Bill looked at me like I was an alien, but told me it sounded like a great idea. He paid me $10 for every shoplifter I caught. I made more catching little thieves than I did on the clock.

## A Teacher

About half way through my senior year Mr. Lewis, my government teacher, cornered me one day as I was leaving class. He said, "Gardner, you can continue down your path of self-destruction, or you can use the leadership talents I know that you have to change the world". I was doing good to change my tee shirt, so why was Mr. Lewis all of a sudden interested in me and my welfare? He asked me if I was planning on attending college. I told him I didn't have the grades or the desire to go to college to learn to sit behind a desk pushing papers for the rest of my life.

Mr. Lewis explained that not all college degrees led to desk jobs. One day he suggested the forestry industry as a career area that might be of interest to me. Mr. Lewis started talking with me about thinking beyond the environment I currently knew.

Mr. Lewis continued his persistence in making me think about my future. I began to realize he wasn't giving up. He saw something in me that I couldn't see. He truly cared about kids and not just teaching them academics, but also teaching them about life skills and changing their game if he could.

My hood was still a challenge for survival. It was 1974, and not more than 150 yards from my mom's house, the first victims of the soon to be nationally famous serial killer, BTK, were found hung from the plumbing pipes of their basement. Bind, Torcher, and Kill was the moniker Dennis Rader wanted to be known as during the 30 years he taunted local law enforcement and the press. His last victim was the mother of a junior high and high school classmate who would ultimately become Rick's second wife. For me as a 17 year old high school senior, even considering the outrageous physically dangerous activities I was involved in, life was still safer staying away from the hood as much as possible.

Mr. Lewis volunteered to help me in whatever way he could during my final semester of high school. I started doing some research on forestry to try to understand what the industry was all about and what careers were available. I also began looking at the related programs in some of the universities in Colorado where dad lived.

**A Whisper:** I had never thought of going to college and here I am researching college and forestry. I heard The Whisper. "Considering all you've been through during the past eight years, is there any reason to fear going to college?"

My extracurricular illegal and otherwise bad behavior began to drastically subside. I didn't have time for it and I was losing interest over new safer and healthier activities  Through all of the illegal and insanely dangerous things I did over the previous eight years, I never got caught for vandalism, assault, arson, under age sex and alcohol consumption, illegal drug use and sale, grand theft, nothing.

I told my girlfriend who was a junior in high school, a year behind me that I was going for it. I was going to college in Colorado. Obviously, this meant that we would be separated for nine months until she graduated and could join me. What a whack job I was. Needless to say, she was not happy about my plan.

I was accepted at Metropolitan State in Denver Colorado. Of the 600 plus graduating seniors in my high school, I was not only going to start college, I was going to start college in Colorado. It was all a bit surreal for this punk who at the time didn't really understand what was happening or why. I was actually beginning to feel my head rising up and my shoulders pulling back. Mr. Lewis had changed my game in less than six months following eight years on what I thought was the Highway to Hell.

Once settled in Colorado at my dad's house, I got a job at the local Mobil service station. My dad decided to build out a room in their basement for me so that I could have a little privacy and a quiet place to study.

Metropolitan State had no campus! Classes were held in various buildings in the downtown Denver area. The area had very familiar sights, aromas, and sounds. The winos were passed out in vacant doorways, homeless folks huddled up with their shopping carts stuffed with their worldly belongings. The stale smells of cigarette smoke, over used grease from the burger and donut dives, horns honking, and sirens screaming. But, now I was on my way to my college classes. My reading was starting to get better simply from practice. It's amazing how that works.

Sometime in early November, I received the cold information that my girlfriend back home had started dating someone else. The news knocked me into left field for some reason. I had never been dependent on anyone! I was also beginning to get a little home sick. Why? I should have been on top of the world. In reflection, my life had changed so drastically so quickly that I felt I had become untethered from anything I had known to be real.

In mid-December it was time to go back to my old world and I was afraid. I was afraid to tell my dad. It had taken me at least two weeks to get the courage to tell him I was leaving. I knew he wouldn't understand and he didn't. I didn't know what I was going back to. Would I fall back into my destructive life?

My mom had moved to a small town with my little sister, but she had not sold the old house. Mom still had the flower child thing going on and Mark was next in mom's batting order. Mark was a potter by profession. When he wasn't smoking pot, he was spinning pots and otherwise made and sold ceramics for a very meager living. Mom's hip little marriage to Mark didn't last too long before mom was off chasing her next prey.

John Turner was a railroader, who was a fair bit younger than mom. The railroad was well known for drug use and trafficking. John's favorite texture and color was fine white powder. As it ended up, he was the last of the test rats in mom's life science project.

Since mom's house was available, I camped out there which made it convenient to try to patch things up with my girlfriend, since she and her parents lived just two doors down.

I headed out to the university Registrar's office with my transcripts in hand. There isn't much call for forestry in Land of Oz, so I registered for engineering classes that would begin in January. Now I just needed to find a job to support myself.

**The Whisper:** I heard The Whisper. "You've come too far to even think about reverting back to the criminal element for money."

My friend John, the high school parking lot wine distributor, had gone to work for a large wholesale pharmaceutical company. John told me they had an opening for a delivery driver. My first day on the job was quite surreal as I was driving around town in an unmarked van delivering everything from cough syrup to pure cocaine. I remember thinking, I'm delivering little glass bottles of the pure stuff that would sell on the street for a hundred times more than the wholesale cost to the pharmacist. Mr. Lewis had invested in me, now I had to continue to invest in myself and not allow thoughts that would lead to self-destruction.

I finally convinced my girlfriend that we should get married after she graduated in May. We married on August 30, 1975 for all of the wrong reasons and divorced just over a year later. Great! What self-respecting girl would ever want to date a 19 year old divorcee?

About that same time, a position in the warehouse at work opened up and I was moved from delivering drugs to managing the narcotics vault. You can't be serious! I was now in charge of what would have been for me a candy store about three years earlier. Rows of cocaine, Percodan, Valium, Demerol, etc., and I was now responsible for inventory with the FDA.

Rick was also divorced and he and I were now roommates. He got my old job as a delivery driver where I worked. We would laugh about the irony of what we had been through together with illegal drugs, having never been caught, and now we were on the legal side of the fence.

I was introduced to computers as part of the engineering program at school. I also knew we had something known as the computer center at work. I told Mike the computer center manager what I was doing in college and that I thought I would like to work in his computer center if there was ever a spot available.

A position became available in the computer center at work. I hadn't worked in there long when it was announced that Mike was being promoted to a facility in Texas. I didn't even have to apply for the manager position. Mike just quickly taught me most of the aspects of managing and operating the computer center.

**The Whisper:** I was 21 years old, running a computer center with people who were all older than me. I heard The Whisper. "Your employees aren't just going to do as you say. You have to learn, sometimes the hard way, that influence, not command and control is the secret to motivate people to perform to their potential."

My experience with remote pharmacy systems caught the eye of Pizza Hut, a company that was founded and headquartered in my home town. I was invited to become part of a team to develop a concept that has become known as point of sale.

## Teacher #2

I began taking a few business classes, one of which was called Entrepreneurship. I wasn't exactly sure what it was all about other than it had something to do with owning your own business.

Dave Carey was professor of the class. For some reason Dave took an interest in me, similar to Mr. Lewis. He had just been named Associate Director of the one of the first Centers for Entrepreneurship on a university campus in the US. Dave was excited about the new center and wanted me to get involved. He introduced me to Dr. Barton, the former Dean of the business school and now Founder and Director of the Center of Entrepreneurship. My home town had long been a hotbed of major corporate startups including, Pizza Hut, The Coleman Company, Rent-A-Center, Beach Aircraft, Cessna Aircraft, Learjet, Koch Industries, and others. Dr. Barton consulted with many of these companies, so why not take advantage of the local business brain trust by offering services to other startup and fledgling companies.

I was surprised to learn that technology was not being leveraged by these business titans. I explained to Dr. Barton that there were little computers from Radio Shack and a small startup company called Apple that could perform the financial modeling the center was providing prospective startups. The work that was being done with TI calculators and ledger pads could be done in a hundredth of the time. Before I knew it, Dr. Barton had me in his car on the way to the local Apple dealer. That day, Dr. Barton bought an Apple II personal computer. He then told me he would pay me to come to his home on Saturday mornings to teach him and his teenage son to use the new computer.

**The Whisper:** Me, a reforming bad boy from the hood teaching a former business school dean who was a PhD to boot? I heard The Whisper. "Had it not been for Mr. Lewis and Professor Dave being strategically placed on the path of your journey, you would never have met Dr. Barton. Therefore, you need to respect the opportunity to simply be a sponge with what you're being exposed to."

My position with Pizza Hut involved constant travel. The days were long and the evenings even longer for a single 22 year old. I could hang out in the hotel bar with cheesy music and women over twice my age. I could watch TV; however this was before ESPN and MTV. All became old quickly.

It seemed to me, if we could connect a microcomputer cash register in a Pizza Hut store to a mainframe computer back at corporate over a simple telephone line, there has to be a way to build a small keyboard device that could attach to the TV and phone line in my hotel rooms and connect to remote computers that could serve up volumes of interesting stuff. This idea rolled around in my head for the next three years.

My passion for business was blossoming and I was learning a great deal helping Pizza Hut develop the point of sale technology. However, my travel schedule made it virtually impossible to regularly attend my college classes.

**The Whisper:** I heard The Whisper. "You know this stuff and you have a good business head. You don't need school right now. Pursue your career and you will never look back."

Soon thereafter, Dave Carey said he had confidence in my knowledge and leadership ability and that he wanted me to consider leaving Pizza Hut. Dave wanted me to become the general manager of a furniture manufacturing and retail business that he owned. He wanted me to help him proceduralize and automate his company.

**The Whisper:** I'm just a 24 year old kid from the hood who doesn't even have a college degree and you want me to run your company and you're going to give me tens of thousands of dollars to implement systems that will change the way you do business? I heard The Whisper. "This teacher sees in you what you cannot yet see in yourself. Plus, it will be a great education."

I left Pizza Hut to join Dave as the GM of his furniture company. I dove in and started learning the operations of a furniture company so that I could begin designing the transformation to automated systems. Even though I wasn't traveling like I had been with Pizza Hut, I was swamped with the transformation project and knew returning to college in the fall was no longer an option.

I happened across a newspaper ad posted by a company in Dallas that was starting up to deliver information over a phone line to an intelligent keyboard. Now that sounds familiar. I sent my resume off and a few weeks later they were interested in talking with me.

Close to the end of my time with Pizza Hut, I was introduced by two coworkers to a friend of theirs from Texas. This young woman would become my second wife and the mother of my children.

On a trip to Dallas to visit my girlfriend, I was interviewed and ultimately hired by the company president. Although I hadn't completed all that I had planned for Dave's furniture company, Texas was calling my name.

I made the move to Big D. My Texas girlfriend and I got married; and soon had a daughter on the way. People say not to change too many things at once. Quitting a job, moving to a new state, starting a new job, getting married, again, and having a baby coming seemed like greatness.

## Teacher #3

Once I joined the new company in Dallas, I learned that my boss and company president had graduated at the top of his class from the US Naval Academy. He became a Marine Captain until he had been hand selected by the CEO of the world's largest computer services company. John Green was only about six years older than me, but he was already a legend.

John immediately took me under his wing. We spent countless nights at the office on whiteboards and flip charts, brainstorming and laying out strategy for the company. Our company built color graphic pages of information about the local area from movie and restaurant guides to shopping and event information. All was accessible from custom public kiosks we designed and built as well as from personal computers like the Apple II and Commodore 64. The technology we delivered was essentially a small precursor to what we now know as the internet.

John rarely put fewer than 90 hours per week into the company. However, I observed something very important to him. John started making phone calls every Friday to ensure that all of the elderly and physically challenged members of his church had a ride for Sunday morning. If they didn't, John made sure they did. There was no question that God and country came first in John's world. I learned more about life and business in one year from John Green than I had learned during my previous 25 years. After a couple of years, John left the company to start a new venture of his own. Tandy/Radio Shack decided to enter the information distribution and retrieval business. I joined them as a product manager.

After several years of coaxing offers from my former next door neighbor and friend, I joined Fidelity Investments. I commuted back and forth from Dallas to Boston, holding several leadership positions over my ten year stay while working with MBA's and PhD's from all of the Ivey League schools. It all seemed surreal and at times overwhelming when I thought about the journey I had traveled so far.

**The Whisper:** I heard The Whisper. "Thanks to John Green and your experience, you've developed the knowledge and capability to hang with and lead some of these highly educated and seasoned professionals. You can do anything you decide to do."

Through my lessons from Mr. Lewis, Professor Dave, and John Green, I began to realize the value and satisfaction of developing people around me to their full potential.

My second and the last of my cool kids was born in 1989. This time it was a son and now I truly felt complete as a father.

When my daughter was 11 years old she was invited by a friend to play in a junior golf tournament. She had never set foot on a golf course. My daughter and her friend were disasters as was the weather that day, but she loved it and said she wanted to learn the game. She spent the next ten years with Hank Haney and his team. She became one of the top ranked junior golfers in the world which earned her a free ride through college. Observing thousands of hours of Hank and his world class teachers develop kids and professional golfers to the world class level has enabled me to use some of the same lessons to develop people around me.

My son is one of those naturally talented people. He is academically intelligent and graduated early from high school although he struggled early with attention challenges. Like father like son.... He's a better natural golfer than his sister, but chose not to indulge in the grind of international tournament play. He is a highly gifted musician, with the ability to play beyond his years on the saxophone and the guitar. My son was a very good wrestler in high school and is now developing as an expert in mixed martial arts while attending college.

In 1997 I was hired by Levi Strauss to lead part of their global IT organization. Over my thirteen year career, I led many of the global IT organizations. For the first time, I had the opportunity to understand and lead people from different cultures around the world. It was a fascinating experience where I learned leadership lessons of a lifetime. Developing people from other cultures was a very different challenge, but was incredibly rewarding.

After a few years of global responsibility where I was never off of the grid, it was time to do something new that would allow me flexibility and hopefully have greater impact. I knew it was time to leave the corporate world and to rekindle my entrepreneurial spirit.

I attended the annual men's conference at my church. At the conference I met and talked with John C. Maxwell for a few short minutes. I had read a couple of his books and knew that he was often referred to as the world's leading authority on leadership. Three days later I received a call from John's office asking if I would be interested in joining The John Maxwell Team as a Founding Member.

**A Whisper:** The caller said she knew I had talked with John and he was forming a new leadership company that would carry on his legacy by speaking, coaching, and teaching his leadership lessons. I heard The Whisper. "This is your purpose. This is why you're here."

It has been one of the best decisions I have ever made. I've met and developed relationships with some of the most amazing people around the world. The experience has opened doors that I had never seen before.

I've seen the illness and felt the pain of today's kids who are in that box that my teachers and The Whisper built the ladder for me to climb out of.

**The Whisper:** I was the worst of the worst when I was the age of these kids. I heard The Whisper. "You've experienced their pain, their struggles, and you have a message to share".

My personal challenge is to help develop the resources to recreate the public education system in our country. This initiative will cause a grassroots, fundamental change in our schools, our families and our communities.

The kids and parents I work with now sometimes ask why I spend my time with them, so I tell them about the teachers and The Whisper in my life. I tell them how Mr. Lewis could have spent his time investing in someone other than me, but thankfully he didn't. I tell them that no matter how bleak their circumstance may seem, there is hope. I let them know that they have an important story and that they have a purpose. I tell them to listen for The Whisper and to look for doors to open.

I've lived it and I just hope to pay it forward, not for me so much as for Mr. Lewis.

Jim Gardner is the Founder/Principal of Legendary Leadership Arts. Jim speaks, coaches, and consults with business and organizational leaders, educators, and students on personal branding, productive organizational culture, and leadership development. Jim's vision is to help his clients identify and execute the critical processes necessary to develop extraordinary personal and organizational legacies.

Jim is first a student of people and organizational behavior, studying why some sustain superior performance, most exist in mediocrity, and others self-destruct. As a certified John Maxwell leadership teacher and speaker, Jim is a master of leadership process and development.

Starting and leading multiple enterprises, Jim has always been an entrepreneur. He has also served for over 30 years as a corporate executive and leader for iconic brands including McKesson, Pizza Hut, Tandy/Radio Shack, Fidelity Investments, and Levi Strauss & Co.

**Jim Gardner, Founder & Principal**
Legendary Leadership Arts
Email: JGardner@LegendaryUnited.com
Website: www.LegendaryLeadershipArts.com

Follow Jim:
www.facebook.com/pages/Legendary-Leadership-Arts/227059283999409
Twitter: @JGardnerTX

# Who Is Driving Your Bus?

By MaLinda Hammond

*This chapter is dedicated to all those who want to have a voice but who are scared to speak up and to those who are unhappy but can't seem to make a change that matters.*

In April 2003, I was headed to Manas AB, Bishkek, Kyrgyzstan on my second deployment. You could say that my first deployment was less than successful. I had been assigned with a new instructor pilot and a challenging engineer. In just over two months at Karshi Khanabad, Uzbekistan I learned very little that would help me prepare for my new assignment. To say I was apprehensive about flying out on this deployment would be an understatement. I felt pretty good about my new aircraft commander but I didn't know any of the other crewmembers.

Thinking back, with a sigh of relief, a few weeks into the deployment, I recall fitting into my new crew when "the light bulb went off." Flying under austere combat conditions is not the same cushier flying that I had experienced during pilot training or at Dyess AFB, Abilene, Texas. There are a lot of new concepts thrown at you during the early stages that you just don't get. I should have had my "ah ha" moment during my first deployment, but due to the circumstances it just never happened. In subsequent years of flying, I have had the pleasure to watch other new co-pilots have their "ah ha" moments. It is almost as if you can see the light bulb go on over their heads.

As any crew member will tell you, after a while no matter how much you like your crew; they are going to get on your nerves. It happened with mine as well. They had been there a lot longer than I had and were starting to get short. I still had about four long months to go after they left.

Our moods weren't helped by the weeks of 10:00 pm alerts. For whatever reason, the schedulers had decided to just leave us on this alert time. This was the worst alert time. It meant that you had to try to go to sleep during the day and then flew all night long. They were supposed to rotate our alert times so that no one was constantly sleep deprived but for some reason they just left us on this schedule for weeks.

My aircraft commander had gone to the scheduler on several occasions and requested to have a later alert so that the crew could get some sleep but they never did. My aircraft commander was the type of person that let things like these get him. He didn't think that he deserved to be treated this way. Once he even made the request to delay our alert time and was totally ignored. He let the internal turmoil overwhelm him. He focused on his anger to the exclusion of everything else.

In addition to this outside influence, the pilot had an ongoing competition with another aircraft commander. They kept boasting over which crew was the "A" team. They started keeping tabs on which crews had 100% mission completion rates. At the time, all of the crews flew every other day with very few days off. Our crews always seemed to fly on the same days. It became normal to have banter going back and forth with a lot of ribbing if someone broke or couldn't make it in because of the weather. In the safety world, we call these outside influences links in the error chain. There would be many.

So about two weeks before my crew was going to go home, we had yet another 10:00 pm alert. The aircraft commander started the day by talking to one of the assistant director of operations (ADO) about the situation. He proceeded to spend the rest of our prep time brooding about the situation instead of paying attention to what was being said during the briefings. Except for the short period of time that the other crew did their usual strutting around the room, bragging how they were the "A" team and were going to fly circles around us. As soon as they left, he reverted back to his dark mood.

The basic crew for the C-130 is comprised of three officers−two pilots, one navigator and three enlisted−one engineer, and two loadmasters. All but the loadmasters are up in the cockpit and all members are on headset and can hear everything that is going on in the plane. For these missions, the officers and enlisted would all sit together and go over each of the airfields that would be flown to on that day. Everyone on the crew would know what to expect for the day. We would look at the specific airfields, the surrounding terrain and any possible threats.

In Afghanistan and the surrounding countries, there is a lot of terrain. We are talking−put a stop to Alexander the Great−kind of mountains here. He rolled over every enemy he faced. Then he ran up against the Hindu Kush and came to a screeching halt. C-130 versus the ground...the ground wins almost every time. So it was customary to spend additional time preparing for our missions to avoid unplanned contact.

On this particular day, we had the normal basic locations that we had been to time and time again. We still reviewed all of our planned airfields and discussed our plans. When the briefs were over, the enlisted made their way out to the aircraft. They were looking over the aircraft and making sure that all of the systems are working correctly. If we had a load going out of Manas, they would have that loaded. The officers stayed inside and discussed in more detail our mission plan for the day.

Just before we were about to "step" to the aircraft, the other crew comes back inside. My commander immediately smells weakness and goes for the throat. Sure enough, they had a mechanical malfunction that was going to prevent them from flying their mission. The ADO made the decision that their mission was more important than ours. He decided that we would take their mission and told us to brief up. You can only imagine all of the gloating that was going on over this one. I mean, not only are we going to finish our mission; we are going to finish YOUR mission. No pressure at all here.

Unfortunately, there was an airfield in Pakistan that no one on our crew had ever been to before. It was in a bowl which means that it was surrounded by high terrain on three of its four sides. We lost one C-130 at Jackson Hole, Wyoming with the same kind of terrain. There had also been a marine C-130 crash in the mountains during an air-refueling mission at this airstrip in Pakistan.

It wasn't ideal to not have our enlisted personnel with us but we sat down and listened to the briefs with the plan to back-brief our other crew members out at the plane. When we told our engineer about the change in plans, he expressed some concern about going into an airfield that none of us had been to before. We thoroughly reviewed the airfield diagrams and charts. We went over the specific terrain and how we were going to fly in and out of the airfield.

We had a few stops before the bowl airfield. Unfortunately, the aircraft commander had a hard time shaking his bad mood. He was so focused on his grievance with the scheduler that he was a bear to be around. He was snapping at all of us and not fully aware of everything that was going on. He would get so focused that his flying went out of the window. It had happened from time-to-time over the two months we had been together, but during the last few weeks it had gotten scary.

As we started to descend into the bowl airfield, we noticed that there was a dusty haze. This airfield had no instrumentations to tell us where we were in relation to the field and consequence to the terrain. Pretty soon we realized that there was a dust storm in the bowl. At about 10,000 feet we could no longer see the mountains or the ground. We should have turned around right then. The engineer started to get nervous and was questioning the necessity of continuing with the mission. But we were the "A" team. We had to successfully complete the mission.

Now this is a good place to introduce my newly assigned navigator. We had a great navigator for most of the assignment, but he had met his deployment limit and was sent home. I had spent the past few weeks completely exasperated in my attempts to work with our new navigator.

We had this fancy 1950's technology radar on our plane. Most navs can use this equipment to find anything. I'm talking runways, cities, mountains, lakes, rivers, you name it. We weren't supposed to use it in the weather for a very specific reason: it was old technology and you could easily "bite off" on the wrong thing or misinterpret what it is you thought you were seeing. But let me tell you, some navs are absolutely amazing with it. Not the new navigator. To complicate matters further, English was his second language, so basic communication was problematic.

Don't misunderstand my comments, I do like navigators. Unlike many pilots, I like having them on my plane. Some feel that they are better off without them. Not me, no sirree. And it has absolutely nothing to do with the fact that my husband is a navigator.

So here we are going into an airfield that is a bowl with very high mountains on three sides; there are no instruments on the field to help us navigate; and we have a navigator who is severely lacking in the skills and communications areas. Did I mention we should have turned back at this point?

We are flying along, descending as we go. The engineer gets a glimpse of mountains off to the left and they are very much higher than we are at this point. He questions the pilot again about if we should be doing this or not. The pilot is completely confident. I remember looking at the engineer. We didn't have to say anything. We were both thinking of the list of incidents recently where the pilot just wasn't all there.

Oh crap, do I say something? You see, I'm just a co-pilot. My job is to shut up and do what I am told. Some of those incidents in the past few weeks were a direct result of me questioning something that the pilot had done. The reactions had been harsh and shut down both me and the engineer. I wanted to say something but what can I say that won't bruise his ego?

Our one saving grace is that we have a navigation system that works off of GPS. If the navigator gets the coordinates right then our system will fly us straight to that point. I double checked those coordinates. I also put them into another location as a back-up.

At some point during the descent, the pilot made the decision to "educate" me on a technique. He took his system from this wonderful navigation system to TACAN. TACAN is just a type of system that is not present on this field. You can, however, move the needle to orient your instrument to the direction of the runway. The pilot did this to have a depiction of the runway. For instance, would he see the runway straight on or at a 90 degree angle? At some point it appeared the pilot completely forgot that he had made this switch. I can't speak for what he was thinking through the whole ordeal but his decisions and actions indicate that he thought he was still on our navigation system and that his needle would take him straight to the field instead of simply showing the orientation of the runway. However, I was still on the navigation system.

We continued to descend and configure the aircraft. Configuring the aircraft means that you are putting the landing gear down and extending the flaps. I noticed that the pilot had a significant vector away from the runway as we continued our approach. He was drifting right and I was giving him feedback that the runway was to the left. However, he did not make any corrections. He was focused on his "TACAN" and convinced that he was on centerline. As we continued, we never did see the mountains or the ground.

At 300 feet we were still in a brown out situation with the dust storm. The engineer called the 300 feet and told the pilot to go around. The pilot continued to descend looking out in front of him to see the runway. I continued to give him updates that the runway was to our left. 250 feet....200 feet...I echoed the engineer by calling a go around. Finally when the engineer called 150 feet and we still couldn't see the ground the pilot initiated the go around. We pulled the gear up and the flaps in and started to climb away.

The pilot asked the navigator to give him an ARA (what does this stand for?) back to the runway. Chirp....Chirp....absolutely nothing from the navigator. There was absolutely no comment or direction at all. The pilot asked three times for the navigator to give him some kind of input with no reaction at all. Finally, I started to give the pilot vectors back around to final. It wasn't the first time on this deployment that I had to do this. At some point we had resigned ourselves to the reality that our navigator was not an effective crew member. So I was forced to vector the pilot back around to final approach.

As we are headed back out, the engineer asks the pilot if this is really the smart thing to do. We never did see the ground and there is really no reason for us to be trying this hard to get into this airfield. Well except for the "A Team" factor. I will never forget this moment. The pilot turned around and looked at our engineer and asked him, "Do you trust me?" Wow, of course we trust him. We had trusted him for the past two months.

To be honest that trust had been wavering over the past few weeks. There had been several instances where we were not sure if he was really there with us or not. His tunnel vision had gotten very bad during the last few flights. But to be put on the spot like that, of course we trusted him. This is the reality. No pilot should ask this question. No crew should accept this question. If you are uncomfortable with the situation, if you are breaking the rules to get the mission done, if the hairs on the back of your neck is standing on end; you get the hell out of dodge.

What followed was my biggest mistake. The engineer was so upset that he removed himself from the flight deck. The pilot called for the flaps and the gear. You don't do this without the engineer. He is calling the checklist and he verifies that the gear is down and locked. Besides, you don't just keep chugging along against your crew members when they are obviously in distress. I was in complete turmoil. I didn't want to be there. I wanted the pilot to abort the mission. I was just a co-pilot and so I kept my mouth shut. I put the flaps and gear down and continued to give the pilot vectors. At some point on final, the pilot stopped taking my input. Once again, he got tunnel vision on his "TACAN", and did not realize he was not on centerline. He was drifting to the right again.

The engineer composed himself and came back to his seat. We both continued to feed the pilot information. At around 200 feet we broke out of the dust and could see the ground. The pilot leveled off and started looking for the runway in front of him. I tried to tell him that he was well right of the runway but he kept his focus straight ahead. Finally he stated, "I can't see the runway." At that point, we were beside the runway. I was totally exasperated and pointed across his chest at the runway and said, "Because the runway is over there." The pilot looked over to his left and immediately saw the runway. He made a turn to the left to fly over the midpoint of the runway.

We normally do low altitude tactical approaches that cross the runway and has a continuous turn to final, and have a count for this based on starting the maneuver at 250 knots. Over the runway you pull your power back to idle. You count for two to three seconds to get enough offset from the runway and then you start your turn to final to land. My pilot was still configured and flying 150 knots. He should have increased his time for offset but he was too focused on getting the mission done. As he crossed the runway, he counted and started his turn too soon. This caused us to overshoot the runway by a large margin.

We were really too low and too far from centerline to safely land the aircraft but he was determined to put the aircraft on the ground. At 100 feet he had an excessive bank angle and was still not on centerline. The engineer called a go around. At 50 feet he was lined up on the lines on the side of the runway and making another aggressive correction back to centerline. I called a go-around. The pilot did not react but continued to try to land. I started trying to push the throttles up and called for the go-around again. The engineer screamed, "For the love of God, pilot, go-around!"

This got through to him. He stood the engines up and started to climb away. When you execute a go-around, you push power towards max. There is no direction on exactly what you have to reach. It is whatever will get you flying safely away. This resulted in only about 75% power. The pilot went into a 45% bank and started pulling the aircraft around for another attempt at landing. There is no reason for this aggressive maneuver. I called out that the aircraft was only at 200 feet. The engineer called the airspeed at 120 knots.

Those hairs on the back of my neck started standing on end again. Very quickly the engineer was calling the loss of airspeed. 110 knots, 100 knots, 90 knots….I was at the controls fighting the pilot to roll the aircraft wings level. He had taken both hands and put them on the yoke. I took the opportunity to push all four throttles to full max.

We were also losing altitude. The engineer changed over to calling the altitude, 150 feet, 100 feet. At this point, the aircraft was in a full stall. At first, the shaking was minimal but quickly changed to a teeth jarring shake. I yelled, "You're in a full stall! Roll out!"

For clarification, a stall is when the plane stops flying. The airflow over the wings gets disrupted. Instead of the air flowing smoothly and thus creating lift; the airflow starts to move in a circular motion. This circular movement of the air is the shaking that you feel. Once you create a smooth airflow over the wing, you will begin to fly again. The wings will create lift and you can climb away from the ground.

The pilot rolled the wings level and shoved at the throttles. There was no more to give. We continued to shake and lose altitude. I was convinced that we were going to be landing this plane out in the desert. So, I started looking in front of us to find a place where there were no buildings, trees, or livestock. We were so lucky that the trees were the stunted trees of dry areas and less than 50 feet tall. In my home state of Alabama, we would have already been in the trees and going down. At some point, we finally stopped shaking and slowly started to fly again.

The pilot made the decision to abort the mission. We made a turn to the west and started to climb out. I contacted tower to let them know that we would not be landing and were going to return to our base. I have no idea what the people in the tower thought of our display. I am fairly sure the visibility was high enough for them to have witnessed this last debacle. At times, I have wondered what it looked like to them and if they knew just how close we had come to disaster that day.

Tower advised us that there was an unmanned aerial vehicle (UAV) at 10,000 feet between 15 and 20 miles from the runway. As we were climbing out, I started to do the math. At our current climb rate, we were going to be flying straight through his flight path. Today, our aircraft have an instrument that will broadcast to other aircraft where we are and at what altitude. We use this to avoid other aircraft. A lot of aircraft have this instrument and they talk to each other and use algorithms to keep us from hitting each other. We didn't have this back then and it wouldn't have mattered because neither did the UAV.

At this point I instructed the pilot to level off at 8,000 feet. The navigator then began yelling at me and told the pilot to continue his climb. Really? Now you have an input? I explained to the pilot that there was a UAV, where it was, and my reasoning for leveling off. He chose to level off and continued his climb when we knew we were past the threat.

We made it back to base and never flew together as a crew again. I am not sure who went to the squadron commander and made the request to not fly but I was relieved when he took us off of the flight schedule. It wasn't common to sit a crew down but I figured he understood that we needed the recovery time. The engineer and I spent hours going over the incident and what we could have done to prevent the situation.

When this was all happening, I never thought I was about to die. I was just reacting to the situation as it developed. As we relived the events and discussed what had happened; we realized just how close we had come to a disaster. It was a very humbling experience. It also changed my perspective on how I would look at flying and my life forever. I would no longer be "just a passenger" in an aircraft or in life. No longer would I just blindly trust someone else to make the right decisions for me.

Flying, just like life, requires you to participate. I had an obligation not just to myself but also to my crew to make the right decisions and to act upon them. We all make mistakes. What makes us different is if we are able to admit to those mistakes, learn from them, and apply what we learn to our lives in the future. There have been many times since this experience when it would have been easier to just go with the flow; to "let life happen" instead of taking charge. It has been my experience that whenever I have done this, I end up in a place that I never wanted to be –like a sand storm in the middle of the desert.

I have also learned that "leading from the front" is less about the number of stripes on your uniform or your position, than it is about applying your skills, talents and abilities to the maximum in order to serve others, and to meet your goals. Leadership can and is both formal and informal, and the situation largely dictates which leadership approach is required. This is true in the military as well as in your professional, personal and spiritual life.

Leadership is also about collaboration and recognizing the potential in others, and then enabling them to get the most out of their God given talents, abilities and gifts. Whether it's helping my niece become a successful young entrepreneur, leading a new business networking group, helping clients achieve their financial goals, or assisting other pilots, friends and colleagues in reaching their "ah ha" moments; I have made a concerted effort to be a connector and a resource to others, and aid them in reaching their goals.

Today, I spend most of my time encouraging people to take charge of their finances and their lives. So many people get into the rat race and do no more than survive from day-to-day. There is so much more to life! You only get one chance. Make your life what YOU want it to be. This requires you to get actively engaged and be present in your day. Know where you spend your money. Have you ever evaluated what really matters to you? Does your spending match your values?

Make sure that you spend your day doing what you love. Most importantly, devote your day to the ones that you love.

I hear a lot of excuses about finances, marriage, and life; but really, some people don't want to acknowledge the mistakes that they have made. Or at least, not have them front and center in a spotlight. Some just don't want to put in the work necessary to make a meaningful change. And yes, there are some that just don't know what to do or where to start. They are unhappy, scared, or apathetic. For me, it took something that scared me to my bones to realize that life happens whether you are ready or not. I challenge you to live life and to not allow life to live you. Today, I drive my bus. Who drives yours?

MaLinda Hammond was born in Southside, Alabama. She started flying as a kid with her dad; started taking pilot lessons at the age of 15 and got her private pilot's license at the age of 18. She received her undergraduate degree from the University of Alabama. While there, MaLinda participated in the Air Force ROTC and received her commission. With over 2500 flying hours, she has been stationed or deployed all over the world.

Today, MaLinda is a pilot for the Texas Air National Guard. She continues to fly the C-130 Hercules. In her civilian job, she is a financial planner. She helps families and individuals navigate the complexities of personal finance.

**MaLinda Hammond**
Email: malinda.hammond@yahoo.com
Webpage: www.malindahammond.com

Follow MaLinda:
www.facebook.com/machfinancial

# What Did I Get Myself Into?

By Cassandra Krumme


*Our story is dedicated to all the transplant patients. Many have their own amazing story to tell. Some have passed waiting for that organ. Others are still waiting. Then there are those like us who have made it to the other side of transplant and living life as normally as anyone else. Star & Rob, Ken & Fran, St. John's Lutheran Church, Barnes Jewish Christian, Susan, Aunt Sandi, and Shelly all get to claim a part of this story. Thank you!!! The Mizirls and Krummes kept the laughter going and we will be forever grateful.*


I used to think that life is what it is. To some extent, that is true. What matters is what you do with your life. But, that was when I was young and had no clue what life was really about. My husband, Scott, was just as sure of himself as I was of me. That's the way you're supposed to be in your twenties. You're not supposed to know you haven't learned what life is really about yet. Never should you worry about life and death.

I was 27 when we saw the first red flag. Scott was leading the effort to plan for our future. We didn't have kids yet but knew they would be coming. He was applying for a hefty insurance policy that required a health check. We were very shocked when our family doctor told us she couldn't submit his liver enzyme levels to the insurance company. WHAT? He's the epitome of health. Scott was very muscular from his dedicated workout regimen. He ate healthfully and drank minimally.

What could possibly be so bad? I had been working in insurance for quite a few years and knew actuarial tables for life insurance had become fairly generous. We knew this was a mistake and our limited medical knowledge was enough to find it. The results were mind blowing. How could he be so sick and not show any signs? This was the beginning of an odyssey to enlightenment we had no idea we needed.

Scott truly was a lab rat. He had liver biopsies, bone marrow tests and countless vials of blood drawn. In one session alone he filled 13 vials. This doctor did know the next step was to a Specialist that dealt with these types of brain stumpers. He too ran many tests, biopsies and the best he could see was the gall bladder shunting. Not the problem that Scott needed fixing but maybe it was the start on the path to wellness. This specialist realized that we needed even more specialized care and sent us to the "Best that can be found in Texas". Wow, we hadn't heard that before. Since this was our 5$^{th}$ Specialist, we went to him with high hopes and low expectations. Thankfully, he only wanted a couple more tests run.

He said, *"I've got good news and bad news."*

Well, that's new, so it's got to be something good…

He said, *"I know what's wrong with you… but not exactly what's wrong with you"*.

He proceeded to guide us through the myriad of liver diseases that Scott fell into and all the various tangents that changed the diagnosis. Finally, he ended with Scott being a trailblazer in liver disease. Blasted over achiever! They don't know exactly what genetically causes this problem but they know how to treat it, to an extent. Okie dokie then, let's follow the jaundiced trail to healing. Scott spent the next year following a regimen that included some interesting medicines while I dove into learning all there is to know about this disease with no name. We're young intellectuals and we can figure things out. Like all young intellectuals, we read. Yes, and like all intellectuals, we found the more we learned, the less we knew.

During that time, Scott swelled like a balloon. May 3$^{rd}$ 1999 was a typical Monday. Scott went to see his specialist for a routine checkup. They discussed how Scott's stomach was more swollen than usual and maybe up the Lasix dosage temporarily. Scott came home but wasn't interested in dinner because he didn't feel well. He decided the barbecue lunch wasn't agreeing with him. I'm enjoying a TV show when the 10:00 news runs a teaser about the giant tornado in Oklahoma. Holy cow! Scott and I are both from Oklahoma originally so this was very close to home. I run to tell Scott what was going on only to find him in the bathroom passed out. I get him to come to and talk to me. Scott tells me he has food poisoning and is miserable. He has fair skin and red hair. At this moment, he is so pale he's transparent. I call the on-call doctor and give the rundown of symptoms. He agrees it's probably food poisoning.

*"You can bring him to the hospital or you can wait until tomorrow and get into Scott's specialist's office."*

With that diagnosis, we stayed home. Scott feels a lot better Tuesday morning. He planned to work from home because it was our anniversary. I was teasing him that he just didn't want to take me out for our 3$^{rd}$ anniversary. He was joking too and promised to keep up with the tornado coverage and let me know when he heard something. I went on to bowling league. I was in the middle of an incredible game when Scott called. I expected he had news about one set of parents or the other. He told me the Specialist said to get to his office ASAP.

I asked, *"Can I finish the game I'm in first?"*

I'm competitive. It's a grave disease that has no known cure.

*"I don't think so. The Specialist said he would send an ambulance if no one was around to bring me in."*

That's when it first hit me. In the deep recesses of my mind, a very scary place, I hear the slamming of a steel door and the feeling of nothing good can come from this. I grabbed my ball and raced home. I didn't change out of the bowling shoes.

The Specialist gave Scott a 50/50 chance to survive. I looked in the hospital room mirror and saw my face age 10 years. Ten years is a lot when you're in your 20's. It was a long night but Scott came through. He was in the ICU for gastroenterology patients. No visitors allowed. I didn't know this until the second day. Scott told me his Specialist left it in the orders to let me in anytime and to stay as long as I wanted. Apparently, Scott's vitals improved when I was with him. Talk about an ego booster! After that, I called my friend to talk and get a handle on things.

She asked me, *"Why are you still there? Why don't you leave him?"*

I simply answered I didn't know I had a choice. This was the first time I almost lost Scott. Little did I know then that there would be 4 more. Scott had esophageal varices that had burst causing him to lose a large amount of blood. This led to months of weekly visits and EGD's to ensure the blood vessels in his throat stay banded to prevent another episode. While I was waiting for the Specialist to come tell me what he found in each procedure, I had plenty of time to think. I wondered why my friend asked me that question. I must have led her to believe I was that type of person. I didn't exactly question God on life but I definitely didn't turn to Him for guidance either. I knew I wasn't the type of person to tuck tail and run but others clearly didn't. I decided then that I needed to up the ante on what I did for others. I was the crazy woman who took the panhandlers grocery shopping. Scott and I began going to church more often. We discovered we actually felt better about what we were dealing with and that we could handle it. Everything happens for a reason became a mantra.

Scott would be in and out of the hospital over the next year. Life would continue as normal as possible. He was on a medicine regimen that would grow to a whopping 56 pills a day. We still worked, played and travelled. Titania, our first child managed to arrive in 2001. Scott had been healthy for the most part. The doctor gave us the rundown of how the disease was going to progress to an eventual liver transplant. He held up five fingers and ticked them off one by one. Everything happened as he said it would. By this time I knew God had a hand in things.

Soon after, Scott's specialist had an incredible opportunity in another state that he just couldn't pass up. So we started travelling to St. Louis to see him while we interviewed many doctors locally to handle immediate treatment issues. Scott's health declined that same year. We settled into a routine of work, school and doctor visits knowing what was ahead but not wanting it to come. Scott missed Titania's 3$^{rd}$ birthday party because he was hospitalized with Ascites. This is the second time I almost lost Scott. I went to the toy store and bought Titania's first bike. Scott had planned to give it to her and teach her to ride. We didn't know he was going to get sick so fast and wouldn't be able to do it. It's funny how the magnitude of a situation can hit at the oddest times. I found myself bawling my eyes out at the store because I had to buy a pre-assembled bike. We just don't do that. Scott only trusts himself to assemble anything. The store staff didn't know if they should ask to help me or call security to escort the crazy lady out.

We soon learned that Scott was going on the transplant list. His liver was turning from fatty to Cirrhotic.

We called our Specialist in St. Louis for a second opinion and more definition of our options. We had officially entered the transplant world where you fill out paperwork, a lot of paperwork. You must spell out exactly your plan of action moving forward. You must state where you will live, how to contact you, who is the one contact the hospital and staff can talk about your condition, your travel plans and time frame needed once you get the call a liver is ready, what your plan is to cover costs, insurance coverage, and your plan to maintain your new liver. They also want your decision about DNR (Do Not Resuscitate), signed, dated and witnessed. On it goes. While stretching your hand to relieve the writing cramps, you have a moment to grasp the reality of what your future may or may not be. The moment passes quickly so the anxiety can settle in as you go home and wait. And wait. Then wait some more. Over the seven years it took to get to this point, we learned that we are either going to laugh or cry. Once you start either, you're not going to stop. We had a better time finding the humor in things.

*I ask, "What's so funny?"*

*"You know how the alien comes out of the guy's stomach in that movie?"*

I didn't.

*"Well, anyway, there's a spoof movie that has a similar scene but its Kermit the Frog coming out of the guy's stomach."*

This movie I know. I'm into comedies not Sci-Fi. I can't stop laughing. We get a frog to commemorate each hospital visit.

The waiting is the hard part. Waiting for Christmas, your 16th birthday, your 21st birthday, and the call that you have a new liver are all very hard things to wait for. We tried everything, or so we thought. We gave more to charities and we talked more openly with friends. Still the months passed and no call. Things happen for a reason.

The new year was chugging along. Scott had his work and that was very important to him. Finally it dawned on us. We realized that all of this couldn't happen to one person without a very good reason. God was using his sledgehammer to get our attention and it finally worked. We also realized we were trying to solve this problem on our own. We never gave up the things we couldn't control to Him. So on Sunday, January 9th, 2005 we did just that. We spoke with our church pastors and asked for their help. They shocked us. They walked us up to the altar and explained what they were going to do. I'll never forget what Pastor Dastch said.

*"Now don't freak out here. It's not an exorcism but we are going to lay hands on you, Scott, and pray."*

We freaked out a bit in our minds while we smiled and nodded our heads yes, let's do this. My intellect was sparring with my faith. Then it happened. I felt the temperature drop. Goosebumps popped all over. I look at Titania, she looks at me, and she has goose bumps too. We look to Scott and his eyes are closed but he is covered in goose bumps. It was a short time, maybe five minutes, as the pastors prayed over Scott and for a new liver. I don't think there were two words from the three of us, but the pastors understood. There are times when intellect is completely useless.

Two days later, Scott worked late and made it home about 6:30. His cell phone rang as he was plating his dinner. Ti and I were already halfway thru ours. It's our transplant coordinator and she tells him to get on a plane to St. Louis. We have twelve hours and the clock starts now. Outwardly, I was calm and going through the motions getting things in order. In my head I was a raging lunatic running Plans A, B, C, D, E concurrently while setting Plans F, G, H, I and J to pick up where A, B, C, D, E fail. The pre-arranged flight with a private pilot was grounded due to fog in St. Louis. We didn't have a backup for this. Scott called a commercial airline to see if they're still getting into St. Louis. Only first class seats available but they were still going. Here was the catch - we had to be at the airport within 45 minutes for the last flight out. I immediately began praying for traffic to clear so we can get to the airport in 25 minutes, park the car, catch the shuttle to the terminal in 10 minutes, get our tickets from the counter, then race to the gate in 10 minutes. Okay, so that didn't happen. It took 33 minutes to get to the airport and 10 minutes to get to the terminal. There was no way we were going to make it, but we raced to the gate anyway. We arrived at the gate stunned to find the plane still there. As we hurried onboard, we learned that the ticket agent had radioed the gate to hold the plane after she heard our story. Things happen for a reason.

Scott and I are quiet most of the flight. Making small talk. It was like we were on a first date and didn't know what to say. Surreal doesn't begin to cover it.

We landed at Lambert Airport and headed to the Metro. A young man sat next to Scott on the Metro and asked if he knew Jesus.

Scott laughed a little and said, *"Getting closer to him every minute."*

The fellow looked perplexed and Scott shared his news. The young man nodded, got up and sat somewhere else. Things happen for a reason.

We made it to the hospital 3 ½ hours after the initial call and they directed us to the transplant floor to prepare for surgery. The nurse came in to collect all the required paperwork. Awhile later, the Transplant surgeon briefed us on what to expect and how often to expect updates on the progress of the surgery.

Surgery was expected to take 8 to 10 hours and 8-10 units of fluid. With Scott being an over achiever, the surgery took 14 hours and close to 12 units of fluid. My faith was really put to the test during the hours I spent waiting. I was armed with two cell phones and an extra battery. I sent updates to our family every time I heard something.

The nurse was trying to get him to wake up and asked me to talk to him. I leaned over him and asked, *"Scott, can you come back to me; I need you to open your eyes."*

He opened his eyes, saw me and smiled as much as he could. I looked at the nurse to see if that was enough of a response for her records to show he woke from surgery. She had tears in her eyes. She told me that watching family wake patients from surgery was the best part of her job. The next morning, Scott's Specialist came in for a visit. No formalities, just a giant bear hug. All of us were elated that this transplant finally came.

Scott exceeded everyone's expectations on how long he needed to stay in the hospital. He was released on day four. Over achievers rock! We couldn't go home to Texas, just back to the hotel.

As luck would have it, the hospital and hotel were across the street from a park, an extremely large park. We don't have parks like this in Texas! It had several museums and a Zoo. We went to the Science Museum and played with the interactive display of transplant surgery. Our laughter went rampant. We ventured over to the Zoo. We were in hysterics because we thought we snuck in a back gate. On the way out we discovered that the Zoo was free like the museums. Laughing made the walk back to the hotel go by fast. The laughter was short lived. Scott's new liver was dying. He went into renal failure, and then the rest of his systems started to shut down. The transplant coordinator came to admitting, put Scott in a wheel chair and personally took him to ICU.

As the morning dawned, it was time for me to head back to the hospital and check in on Scott. My husband is dying in the hospital and I was alone. My friend's question from long ago came back to me.

"Why didn't I leave?"

A saying I heard often as a kid came to mind fast and at the expense of any other thought.

"No one ever said life is fair. You don't get to quit when the game isn't fun."

I laughed at myself. I laughed hard. I can walk, eat, and sleep. I can do just about anything I want, but Scott can't and this is what I'm thinking about. At that moment, I knew it might take a while but he'll be just fine.

When I returned to the hospital, they were trying to induce Scott into a medical coma. He was fighting it. I told the ICU staff that I don't think this is a good idea and asked they stop. The nurse had to follow the doctor's orders and the ICU doctor refused my request. They tried for a few hours until they were at the maximum dosage and Scott was still opening his eyes trying to talk to me. The transplant team came through on rounds, saw the situation and had the coma stopped.

That night, the ICU doctor came to Scott's room, read the vitals chart and checked Scott. Then he turned to me and said all that matters now is keeping him comfortable. I didn't take this as "the end is near" speech. I knew it wasn't. He said the same to the family of the patient next door. You don't intentionally eavesdrop, but you can't help but hear bits and pieces of conversation around you especially in a hospital.

The next morning, I walk down the hall past the waiting room and navigate around a group in tears. At the end of the hall before the doors to ICU, I see the same family members from the room next to

Scott. They lost their loved one early that morning. That's when it hit home. Scott might not make it. In my despondency, I walk into Scott's room and there he is. He opens his eyes, looks at me and waves. It was a flick of his fingers but it was enough. Debbie comes in after her briefing with the night nurse about Scott's care. She noticed a difference in Scott's vitals. She tells me it's interesting how his vitals improve when I'm in the room. There it is again, that ego boost.

I called Pastor Datsch in what I think was a scream for help. He calmly had me stop, listen to him and follow him in a prayer. I'm convinced Pastor Datsch had God on speed dial.

A song came on the hospital radio. It was new to me and it stopped me in my tracks. It was "Live Like You Were Dying" by Tim McGraw. The words were impactful. Yes, life does stop on a dime. Then it begins moving again with a lot more patience. Little frustrations are just that, little. Scott happened to be awake at the moment and was staring at me. He was communicating with me by writing.

He wrote, *"I love you. I think I'm ready."*

I said, *"No, you're not. You're going to have to trust me and believe me when I tell you you're not done here yet. The doctors aren't giving up on you, I'm not giving up on you and Titania isn't giving up on you. You don't get to give up either."*

My sister, Michel, called to say, *"Okay, Marty is ready to donate"*. Marty is her husband. I got off the phone and realized what she said. I'm hitting call back as fast and hard as I can. So hard, the phone flies out of my hand and lands on Scott's bed, he looks at me like I've lost my mind.

*"Well yeah, where have you been the past week!"*

175

The transplant team walks in. Chuckle and say how they love coming into this room because there's going to be something funny going on. They tell us they have a match. They aren't promising to use it yet. The surgeon is being extremely picky about the liver he's putting in Scott. He doesn't like going back in twice on a patient but they hate losing a patient more. So he's going to check the liver himself.

This time surgery only lasted 12 hours. The liver is beautiful and working perfectly. Scott only needed 10 units of fluid. Thank goodness, he finally laid off the over achiever stuff.

By the time I get to his room, Scott was already awake but Debbie said he's been asking where I am. He's back and cantankerous. All is right with the world again. His complaining was the sweetest thing he could have done for all of us and we were so happy to hear it.

Again, he recovered quickly and was moved to the transplant floor. The over achiever was back. There were no private rooms there. I didn't intentionally eavesdrop but couldn't help but hear some things and strike up conversations with our roommates. I heard one family talk about giving up a car and turning off one of their cell phones. I didn't want to hear more so I walked out in the hall. I had to dodge the news crew that was bringing another patient's plight of trying to pay for his transplant surgery to the evening news. Another family was selling candy bars to raise money. Only transplant patients were on this floor and we were all here for the same reason. Light bulbs started going off in my head and the mustard seed was planted - I need to start helping transplant patients.

We were released to go home to Texas. The fun, however, wasn't over yet. Scott's platelets fell extremely low. He was transfused with platelets twice before we could return home.

Scott had a PICC line to administer medicine. The night they took it out, I don't know what woke me up but I heard a sound. It sounded like a dog that had something caught in its throat. I looked and saw one dog asleep and the other dog standing next my side of the bed. The sound was still happening. I turned to look and saw Scott's side of the bed empty. I flew through the door and found Scott slumped on the sofa. He was stuck on, *"He, he, he, he, he, he, he,"* I tried to get him to respond but he didn't. He just stopped the sound. He was looking at me but he wasn't there. I grabbed the phone and called 911. The paramedics arrived at the same time Scott started coming around. He looked confused and asked "why are all these people in the house?" The EMT's started doing the checks to see what kind of treatment they needed to start. Scott kept complaining about pain. Neither EMT could set a vein to administer pain medicine. They took him to the nearest hospital for a suspected stroke.

It wasn't a hospital that treated transplant patients and the fight to treat Scott began. I felt like I was negotiating a peace pact. The Dallas hospital wanted him transferred there. The St. Louis hospital wanted him transferred to St. Louis. Scott wanted to stay where he was. He had pain medicine and all was right with his world. I stopped both hospitals from transferring him. I promised to get him to St. Louis as soon as he was stabilized.

"You're back!" Everyone said.

I mean EVERYONE in St. Louis said it. We were so well known at that hospital. We expected someone to hand him an I.V. and me a cup of coffee.

The transplant group tried to ease our fears that all is well with the liver. These things happen to transplant patients. Although not to the same patient, still those were common things that happen. Scott regretted being an over achiever, but on the upside, he got another frog.

In August 2005, he finally was hospital free for the first time since January 2005. Life moved on and in July 2006, Branna joined our happy family.

Scott was given a probable 20 years. That sounds like a life sentence. We couldn't have been more excited to have that life sentence. Of course the humor in it for us, in year 20 he's going to live on the wild side. He is seven years old now and we are living each day to the max. We have every day frustrations like everyone else. We live in Texas. Someone is going to cut us off on the highway. That however falls into the little thing category and is forgotten soon. We are works in progress, so the Odyssey continues. Beginning with the adjustment of friends on Facebook who said I could do this. Ha! Just kidding. For me, I have learned that you never know what you are capable of handling until you are thrown into it. This is what came of the mustard seed we were given. Life isn't just what it is. It's what you make of what God gives you.

*** 

I was asked to write this story to show how I became an inspiration to others. Honestly, my first thought was, my friend John is completely nuts. The only inspirational thing I've ever said is "Get off your bum and do something." I tell Scott to get ready for a laugh. He doesn't laugh. Instead he says,

*"Congratulations! You'll be great!"*

*"WHAT?!"* I reply.

It's kind of loud in our family. I decide Scott is too close to the story to be objective. I need to ask a more discerning group. Naturally, I post on Facebook and ask if I should do this. I knew these people would totally get the humor in it and say *"No, not a good idea for you."* As you've probably guessed, I need to re-evaluate my FB friends because not a single person said don't do it. We are works in progress, so the Odyssey continues. Beginning with the adjustment of friends on Facebook who said I could do this. Ha! Just kidding.

The strongest lesson I took from this ongoing life experience is because I can I should. Taking the panhandlers I met grocery shopping was only the beginning. I have a knack for connecting people. I came back from St. Louis with a mission: Help others. The first non-profit I worked with worked directly with transplant patients in meeting their financial needs. The sole fundraiser this group had was a golf tournament. I was able to connect them with a title sponsor for the tournament and they are now on the on the national charitable golf tour. I spent the short time my girls were in pre-school helping them raise funds. When the girls started school, I discovered the myriad of fundraising ventures at public schools. Naturally, I said yes when asked to do something. That moved quickly to the biggest fundraising event in town. I served as auction chair; trying to learn as much as possible from the experience. I met many people who do this for a living. I learned so much about raising the bar. Each stop on this mission has taught me something new. I most recently worked with a non-profit that serves mentally disabled adults as they age out of the school system. I served as the golf chairperson. Interesting tangent here, I have tried golf because my husband was a golfer prior to his transplant. I stink at golf. Like other competitive people, patience isn't a strong suit when trying to learn something new. You need a lot of patience when golfing, a lot of patience. I don't golf. I love the outdoors and being with golfers.

Cassandra and Scott have been married 16 years. Their hobbies and life revolve around their two girls Titania and Branna, two extremely professional watchdogs and an amazing circle of friends in North Texas. Their small community is a hotbed of sports excitement, especially during Football season. However, the Krummes follow soccer, volleyball, basketball, archery and softball just as intently. Music is a passion. On any given day you will hear strains of Tchaikovsky, bumped by Salsa and Hip Hop. With the Eagles, many country flavors and we can't leave out the classic rock; the music selection is very eclectic here.

**Cassandra Krumme**
Email: cassandra.krumme@hilburnpartner.com

Follow Cassandra:
www.facebook.com/CassandraKrumme

# A Grounded Pilot

## By Elizabeth McCormick

*This chapter is for everyone who has had to change their dream while in mid-flight.*

*This chapter is personally dedicated to my daughter, Adara. For the woman you're becoming is as beautiful and strong as the little girl I describe in this chapter. I'm proud of you.*

As I stood on the flight line, the vast expanse of flat land at Katterbach Army Airfield where the Black Hawk and Apache helicopters were parked in front of their respective hangars, I sniffled and blew my nose. I turned to Bill, my Pilot in Command for the upcoming flight and said: "Darn this summer cold! Let's get this preflight done and get going."

Bill was the Pilot in Command, but as a lieutenant assigned to the higher level command brigade, he did not fly often. The operations officer paired him with me for a day of flight training. I was the most experienced co-pilot the unit had, and most likely would ever have.

I had come so close so many times to achieving my Pilot in Command, a status that was the next step in my career, a status that could lead to being an instructor pilot or a maintenance test pilot. My hopes were still up there in the blue expanse of that sky – hopes that I resiliently clung to for my sake and for that of my young daughter. But that "summer cold" would soon signal another battle, one that would require all my strength to carry on.

At Fort Drum, N.Y., my first duty assignment after flight school, I was up for my Pilot in Command check ride. A check ride is like a final exam, where you "act" as the Pilot in Command for a flight with an evaluation flight instructor who monitors and evaluates your every move and determines your performance on a pass/fail basis. Check rides are common. You have an annual performance check ride in your birth month. Any time you fly a new mission, you fly with an instructor pilot. Any time you have an incident, you re-check with an instructor pilot. You work with the instructor pilots every day.

I was at Fort Drum for 2 1/2 years and didn't make my Pilot in Command. I was up for it several times, but while I was stationed there, I was verbally, emotionally and physically abused as well as stalked by a pilot I had dated. Every time I was terrorized, I was yanked off flight duty pending a "psych" evaluation to make sure I wasn't too fragile to fly. The civilian psychologist on base would schedule my appointment for two weeks down the road. No flight time until I was cleared. Over and over and over.

It didn't matter that it wasn't my fault; I had to deal with it. My unit in Fort Drum was hesitant to schedule me for upcoming missions. What if I was attacked again and had to be pulled from the mission, leaving them short-staffed? What if I wasn't back on flight status and fit for duty? My flight time dwindled significantly.

An attack occurred almost every time I was up for the Pilot in Command evaluation to receive my pilot advancement. With each attack, my check ride had to be postponed.

So, I was the most experienced co-pilot – Ever. You see, as a pilot, being the Pilot in Command is the next step in your career progression. You can't get to be an instructor pilot, or a maintenance test pilot until you're a Pilot in Command. Not making Pilot in Command status meant I couldn't progress in my career.

I was eventually re-assigned to Germany for my own safety. The violence had escalated and continued until the week I left the base.

I breathed a sigh of relief to have escaped with my life, but I didn't realize the stigma of being sent to my second duty assignment without that coveted Pilot in Command status. I was perceived as less valuable because I didn't have the flight time commanding my own helicopter. I was once again at a disadvantage.

A new duty assignment involves a lot more for a pilot than for the average soldier or officer. Everyone goes through the standard entry process for any Army base, called inprocessing. You receive a checklist and go all over the base establishing yourself at your new home. It's a lot like enrolling a child in a new school. Old personnel records transferred? Check. Medical records? Check. Housing? Check. Pilots add their unit's flight processing to the list, starting with setting up maps of the region and studying every detail, down to the poles and wires that are a helicopter pilot's biggest worry.

Settling in also included a visit to the flight surgeon, the "flight doc," to establish our medical records there and be reviewed for any changes in medical condition. We all wanted to hear the flight surgeon pronounce us "FFD," Fit for Flight Duty. For some pilots, this initial visit and the birth month flight physical would be the only time they'd see the doctor, even if they were sick. Pilots usually had skinny medical records. Every visit to the flight doc was another chance that we wouldn't be able to fly; for the flight doc to find something that would change a FFD to a DNIF, "Duty Not Involving Flying" status. Never mind that the flight doc's job was to keep us healthy to be able to fly. This wasn't a logical fear, just a realistic one!

We would sit down with the flight instructors, the standardization pilots, who would review our flight records from our last unit and set up our orientation and orientation flight. We knew how to fly the

Black Hawk, but we didn't know the terrain. We didn't know the flight rules for the ranges and airspace. And these rules were different in Germany than they were in the States.

I was good at learning. I picked things up fast and it was a point of pride that I could become an expert on anything I set my mind to. If I was going to be a co-pilot, I would be a darn good co-pilot! I would give it my "all" every day and prove to the instructor pilots that I could be a Pilot in Command.

So in late August 1999, on a beautiful clear summer day, I stood on the flight line with Bill in high anticipation of our flight. I was hand-selected for this flight. The operations officer was instructed to pair Bill, who didn't fly much because of his job, with the strongest co-pilot we had. That was me.

We walked in tandem around the Black Hawk, going through the checklist, looking at every component from the nose compartment to the tail and back around the other side to the nose. Everything looked good. While the crew chief was checking the fuel sample and preparing the aircraft for flight, we reviewed our flight plan, which Bill said would take us toward the Black Forest, by Neuschwanstein Castle and west toward Munich airspace before being back to Katterbach.

"Glad I brought my camera," I tell Bill. "Think we can circle the castle a couple times for some shots?"

"Zoom lens right? Although it's not a no-fly zone, the Germans won't want us getting too close," Bill replied.

"Big lens" I said.

Bill said, "Only if I get copies of the shots." I smiled, sneezed and blew my nose again. "You OK?" he asked.

"Summer cold. I'll be OK," I replied.

184

Only I wasn't OK. Oh, the flight that day went fine and the pictures were beautiful. But that summer cold wouldn't go away. When the stuffy, runny nose (how can it do both?) and sore throat dragged on for weeks, I found myself in the basement waiting room at the flight doc office. It was the start of what would eventually be a career-ending injury for me, an illness that would test my strength but never my resolve.

The flight doc asked me about my symptoms, then handed me a prescription for Sudafed and Cepocal cough drops, both on the approved list for pilots to take while flying. He told me to come back in two weeks if I wasn't better.

By early October, my symptoms had worsened and I had a mild fever and a diagnosis of an easy-to-treat sinus infection. It came with a prescription for antibiotics and a DNIF.

Just as I started feeling better, the antibiotics ran out. Every day off the medicine, the symptoms crept back. I spent most of my off duty time lying on the couch, playing Barbies™ with my precocious 4-year-old daughter, Adara. I was a single parent stationed overseas. Other than my daughter, everyone I loved was an expensive long-distance phone call away.

Back to the flight doc office. "Let's get you on a month of antibiotics this time, order a CT scan, and see if we can get rid of this infection," he said. All I could think was another month without flying? I was taken off my unit's flight schedule and given more desk responsibilities to free up other pilots. My unit was already deployed to Kosovo, and I had been left behind. Hand-selected by the battalion commander to take over the Staff S-4 position for logistics and supply, I covered company and battalion duties and worked long hours every day. Even on the heavy antibiotics, my symptoms slowly worsened. As my body was fighting off the infection, my appetite weakened. The mild headache degraded into a constant throbbing pain behind my eyes and in my ears.

My energy was depleted. Getting out of bed was a struggle. Moving through a day took all the willpower I had. I would pick up my bright, energetic and bubbly daughter from daycare on base at the end of the day, pull through the Burger King drive thru and let her choose from the kids menu. We'd drive the 15 minutes from Katterbach to the officer housing area in the nearby town of Ansbach, my hands shaking on the wheel from exhaustion and my head pounding behind my eyes so wildly that it was hard to focus on the road.

My beautiful daughter would chatter about her day and this friend or that friend, her bright hazel eyes beaming up at me through her thick plastic-framed glasses. She would eat her chicken nuggets and share her life with me, having a conversation much more adult-like than most 4 year olds. It was just the two of us, as it had been for a long time. I'd park my bright blue Pontiac Sunbird in our parking slot and Adara would gather her pink Barbie backpack and walk with me up the stairs. The entryway steps and one flight of stairs felt like a mountain that had to be conquered. The deeper the infection became, the harder it was to walk up those 22 steps. I climbed them with the slow measured step of the infirm.

Robyn or Wayne, the neighbors right below my apartment, would sometimes hear us and open the door with a friendly smile. Later, they would help carry my things up the stairs and even give me a push with a hand under my elbow or on my back.

Reaching the front door was a relief. I would collapse on the couch in exhaustion. Adara would sit next to me and finish eating her dinner while watching a VCR movie. She would wake me when the movie was over to help her bathe and get ready for bed. I would lay next to her, reading her a book and fall asleep before her. After often waking up late for the start of the workday, I learned to leave my alarm set for the next day before Adara's bedtime.

Thus became my routine as I waited and prayed for the antibiotics to start working.

My health continued to decline. As I shuffled into the flight doc's office for my 30-day follow-up, he looked at my pale, almost ashen complexion, and the gingerly way I walked. And without looking at my medical records, he said, "You're not better" and wanted to know why I hadn't returned sooner. "You told me to give it 30 days. Sir," I told him. He checked my vitals and my temperature, 99.9 degrees. My ears were reddened. My nose had stopped running completely. But the pain behind my eyes and in my forehead was so severe I could barely open my eyes.

He suggested we try acupuncture and he applied 10-20 of the silver micro-needled pins into my face and my hands and left me to relax. In my drained state, I immediately drifted to sleep, and seeking a comfortable position rolled to my side. Ting, ting, ting. Half the silver pins fell out of my skin and rolled onto the floor. When the doctor returned, he found me sound asleep. After gently waking me, he walked over to the big computer monitor on the desk and started typing in a referral. It was time to see an ENT and he told me to call Wurzburg Army Hospital the next day to make an appointment. Wurzburg was 90 minutes away and the soonest I could get an appointment was December 14, almost a month away.

This second month of waiting was even more painful than the first. My low-grade fever was a permanent partner. The energy waned more and with the unit deployed, my work load was heavier than ever.

When the freezing cold day of December 14 arrived, I dragged myself out of bed, hopeful for the appointment with the specialist. A light misty rain had started falling as I dropped Adara off at daycare and headed for the Wurzburg Army Hospital. The thin rain combined with the freezing temperatures turned the road into black ice. I left extra early to be sure to get there on time with the treacherous road conditions. Two hours later as I arrived in the outskirts of Wurzburg, I sighed and flexed my tense hands in relief. "Almost there."

And as I navigated down a hill that ended at a stop sign lined by cars, my tires hit a patch of ice and my Sunbird started sliding toward the row of cars. Despite my best efforts, my bumper kissed the bumper of the local German man in front of me. He jumped out of his car and stepped back to survey the damage, screaming at me in German. And although I had learned a lot of Deutsch, in my state I couldn't follow him. I also surveyed the damage. My front license plate screw had scratched his rear bumper. I breathed a sigh of relief at the minor scratch, but that was short-lived as he started speaking in German again and I deciphered the word "polizei."

"Nien polizei, bitte." No police please, I implored him. I reached into the car with my shaky and cold hands, pulled out my wallet and withdrew all the Deutsch Marks I had, worth about 200 U.S. Dollars. "Nien polizei, bitte."

I was in tears. If he called the police, I would miss my appointment, let alone whatever those circumstances would be. He looked at me, counted the money, looked at his bumper and said, "OK American" before getting into his BMW and driving away. I swallowed the tears and hurried to get to the appointment on time.

I walked as fast as my health allowed into the hospital and made my way up the stairs to the ENT clinic. Breathing heavily, I leaned on the check-in counter. "Reporting for my appointment with Dr. Bruce."

"Oh Chief," the specialist exclaimed. "Didn't anyone call you?"

"No," I whined, still out of breath, "Why?"

"Dr. Bruce called in sick today. We'll need to reschedule your appointment."

Despite being on duty in uniform, I couldn't hold back the tears, big fat tears sliding down my cheeks. The young African-American specialist just looked at me, the pilot bawling in front of her. I crossed my arms over the medical records on her counter and laid my head down and sobbed. I felt a hand sternly on my shoulder and heard a brisk female voice behind me ordering me to come with her.

I picked up my pounding head and looked behind me at the female lieutenant colonel I had never met before. I started crying harder as I thought, "now I'm in trouble for crying in uniform."

In her pale blue office, she held out her hand for my medical records while the hot tears tracked down my cheeks. With the door shut, she softened her demeanor towards me and asked what was going on.

I told her, while mopping up my face. She flipped through the medical records. "Well, I'm not an ENT but it looks like your doc should have requested an emergency appointment instead of a routine one," she said. "You should have been seen a month ago. I'm going to walk you downstairs with your records and we're going to declare an emergency and you're going to get seen right away by a German doctor in your own town. OK?"

Two days later, I had an emergency appointment with an ENT right down the street from my apartment. The older, gray-haired doctor clucked his tongue over my medical records and CT scan films I had brought from Wurzburg. "Here, here, here and behind this eye, solid infection. I can fix, must be done soon."

Four sinus cavities impacted with infection. No wonder I felt so bad. "We'll schedule surgery. You'll be in the krankenhouse for five days." Five days! It was almost Christmas.

I was scheduled for surgery 11 days later, to be admitted the night before and then would remain in for four days for surgery and post-op care. I arranged for Adara to stay with Anna, my night childcare provider.

And I prayed that this would fix it.

After the surgery, I felt like a new woman, except I couldn't hear well out of my right ear. It was like hearing through water, an ear full of water with a high-pitch ring and dizziness. Something else was very wrong. I thought I just needed to heal and had my convalescent leave extended from one week to three. But when my energy started coming back and I still had issues with my right ear, the pilot in me knew this was trouble.

I was cleared to go back to work. I was still Rear Detachment S-4, the unit was still deployed to Kosovo, and the work had piled up. I told myself and anyone that asked: "I just need to heal from the surgery." And, "I'll be good as new." I was lying to myself.

On February 8, I was back to the flight doctor with another sinus infection. Twenty-one days of meds this time.

My energy was coming back, but the dizzy spells at night were the worst. They started robbing me of my sleep. Exhaustion crept back.

At work, we were preparing for the return of all the troops and equipment as another unit was moving in to replace our 2-10 Aviation Task Force Falcon in Kosovo.

I had to coordinate the flight schedule, the manifest, the buses to bring the soldiers from the airfield to the base, the equipment and weapons turn in procedure, and to get this all done as quickly as possible so our soldiers could go home to their families. The Rear Detachment Team under my guidance white-boarded the process over and over. How can we make it faster? How can we make it smoother?

I had to fly to Kosovo to handle pre-inventory of the physical equipment and weapons to make sure everything was tagged to come back and that serial numbers matched before the travelling back. Adara, almost ready to turn 5 and start kindergarten, stayed with Anna again.

Although my sinus infection had improved, I was still having the ear issues. The flight doctor referred me back to Dr. Bruce and over the next seven months, I was prescribed nose sprays, ear drops, oral medications, had another CT scan, an MRI and PE tubes inserted into my eardrums to rule out a physical issue with my middle ear.

Meanwhile, the unit was redeployed back home, and I was no longer needed at the battalion level. I became the "fill in" for every able-bodied pilot who had officer watch duty. On officer watch, the base's junior grade officers take turns with a night shift, during which they drive around base in their personal vehicles checking on gates, buildings and the perimeter of the airfield on a regular schedule.

I would put Adara over at Anna's house to sleep for the night while I worked. I was still not sleeping well, and after pulling 3-4 nights a week at this duty, my sleep patterns were temporarily destroyed. The fatigue combined with driving at night was a challenge with the vertigo I was suffering. One night, I was blinded by an oncoming car during a heavy rain and had difficulty recovering with the vertigo spinning in my head. I ended up in the soft mud on the side of the road, thanking God I hadn't hit anyone.

My next appointment was with a neurologist at Landstuhl Regional Medical Center. I didn't trust myself to drive so I took the shuttle bus on the five-hour drive the day before my appointment and stayed on base.

The Air Force Doctor looks over my paperwork, my EEG results, and taking his glasses off, peers at me over his intertwined fingers. "Why are you wasting my time?" are the first words he says to me.

All I could think to say was "I beg your pardon, sir?"

"Your ENT knows you have Meniere's disease. Why is he sending you to me?"

"I'm a pilot, sir. Meniere's is a kiss of death for my career. Is there any chance it's anything else?" I was numb to it by now. I was exhausted.

"It's in your records now," he briskly said as he wrote in my files. He handed me the medical records and dismissed me.

In that five-minute appointment, my flight career was over. I rode the shuttle bus back to Katterbach in a fog and reported to my commander, Captain Sandoval.

He suggested a transfer to a desk job in flight ops. All I could think is – Really? I'd have to watch everyone walk by me every day to fly. I don't think so.

At my follow up appointment with Dr. Bruce, I told him about the dizzy spell while driving and how I was the duty officer filling in for every one of our unit's able-bodied pilots on call. He looks at me concerned, and said, "You shouldn't drive anymore."

"What?! It only bothers me a night. Can we just have it so it's not at night," I asked, panicked that I would lose transportation.

The answer was no.

I sighed and, in an uncharacteristically snide mood, replied, "Well the command is talking about getting me trained and moved to a desk position, but all I've done is fly. What happens if I get vertigo at a firing range? Or while deployed?"

"You're right! You can't fire a weapon either which is a dismissible condition," Dr. Bruce replied. "I'm going to recommend we start your medical evaluation board for discharge."

During the seven months that followed riding the bus to and from work every day or catching rides with friends, the military machine grinded through my paperwork and court paperwork started arriving from Michigan. My ex-husband was suing me for custody in a Michigan court. Adara and I were Texas residents. The Soldiers and Sailors Relief Act of 1940 protects service members from civil proceedings while stationed overseas. Adara was 5, in kindergarten and her father rarely called or sent letters. He had never in the two years we were in Germany come to visit and had even quit paying his child support, making it impossible for me to afford plane tickets from Germany to Michigan. The JAG office sent letters to the court on my behalf that it was illegal to file this paperwork against me in court while I was stationed overseas. The court paperwork kept coming.

The JAG lawyer advised me to call home to Texas and arrange a meeting with a lawyer there straight from the airport to re-establish jurisdiction in Texas.

As soon as I scheduled my flight home, I hired a high-powered lawyer in Texas and set up my first appointment. I sent resumes through email from posting in this "new" job website, www.Monster.com. Within a week, I had a request for an interview, which I scheduled for two days after my return.

Packing. Preparing to move. The movers. Selling the car I could no longer drive. The list to do was long and I was ready to go home. I called my Dad, who lived in Dallas with his third wife and his teenage stepdaughters. "Dad, can Adara and I stay in your guest room while I interview? I don't want to get an apartment until I get a job. It makes sense to get one close to work."

"Should be OK. Can't wait for you to be home." It had been more than two years since I had seen my father or any of my family.

April 13 arrived, and it was time to fly home to Dallas. Adara and I checked out of the same hotel we had lived in when we arrived and boarded the shuttle for the airport.

Because of the time zones, we arrived home at almost the same time we had left, navigated through customs and immigration and met my Dad at the international arrival area.

After a big hug for Adara and me, he loaded our bags into his truck. He looked at me cautiously and cleared his throat, saying "There's been a change in plans."

"Oh, yeah?" What now was all I could think? I just wanted to sleep before I had to meet with the lawyer tomorrow and interview for a job the next day.

"Shari doesn't want you to stay in the guest room. She's afraid having you and Adara there might be too disruptive for her teenage daughters."

"But **I'm your** daughter." I felt like a baby, but I had been away from family for so long and now was going to have to stay in a hotel. I hadn't budgeted or planned for that and I still needed to buy a car. "Whatever. We'll stay in a hotel." I turned away from my father with a hurt expression.

"Your Grandma is in Michigan visiting family and said you can rent her condo."

"Great." Still hurt and thinking of my finances, I turned away from my father and checked on my ball of energy, Adara, who had fallen asleep in her booster seat from the jet lag. I had lost my military career. I had lost my flight status forever. And now I couldn't even stay with my own father, but I was home.

Six months later.....

Most of the time you don't know the blessings of the situation you're in. So many times you may never know the blessing from that difficult period in your life.

It only took six months for me to know that my career-ending injury was God's gift to me.

You see, I nailed that job interview three days after arriving home and secured that inventory accountant position with the experience I racked up while on medical hold. I was able to get us into a nice apartment for Adara to start school.

By immediately securing a lawyer in Texas and borrowing money from family, friends, and my credit cards to pay for it, I was able to fight my ex-husband's request for change of jurisdiction and custody and keep Adara with me.

The fateful day of September 11, 2011, happened and the world stood still and silent while watching the towers fall and the Pentagon burn. And as Americans we'll never feel safe in our own country the same way.

A month after September 11, the unit I was with in Germany was spooling up for deployment. Having been assigned to Rear Detachment duty during the Kosovo deployment, I would not have been spared during this next one. If I had deployed, I would have had to send Adara to live with her father during that expected yearlong deployment. I would have lost custody of my only daughter, as I think he would have used my deployment against me to keep her with him.

And a week after our national tragedy, my neighbor set me up on a blind date. She assured me that he liked kids, although he had never been married and didn't have any of his own. Come to find out — we were both from Michigan and grew up not an hour apart. Six months later, we married, and now we've been married 10 years.

As hard as it is to do, it's not our place to question why things happen. It's human nature to ask it, of course.

But there's a message in that mess you're going through. There's something you're supposed to learn. Sometimes it's a painful lesson, it's an opportunity to build strength of character or will. In my injury, the beautiful gift I received was the opportunity to keep my beautiful daughter WITH ME and not lose custody. As important as I thought my flight career was, when I was faced with the knowledge of what could have been, I cried and praised God for that gift. And now that she is almost 18 and has grown into a smart and beautiful young woman who is coming into HER OWN power, I'm so thankful that I was able to be a mom for her, that I had the means to fight for her in that custody battle and not be deployed so I could be her mom.

Looking back at your challenges, can you see the gifts you were given? I hope you do.

And if you're going through those challenges right now, you can get through anything. You CAN! Believe in yourself and know that you won't be burdened for more than you can handle. You're stronger than you realize!

Much like inprocessing when you first arrive at a new duty station, there are times in life when you have to do the same. You start from where you are. You start over and build on what you have, the good or the not so good. YOU get to choose where you go from there.

 Filmed for the ABC News show "20/20," seen on MSNBC and in the Wall Street Journal, Elizabeth McCormick has empowered audiences all over the USA with her inspirational speaking. A dynamic entertainer, Elizabeth keynotes from main stages sharing the challenges faced in her years as a Black Hawk Helicopter pilot and empowering audiences with the stories coupled with actionable lessons.

Black Hawk Missions Elizabeth has flown:

- Air Assault/Rappelling
- VIP
- Command & Control
- Military intelligence-gathering flight plans

In 1999, Elizabeth supported UN peacekeeping operations in Kosovo as the Battalion S-4 overseeing the logistics of deployment and coordinating the return of all soldiers and property at the deployment's completion.

She was medically retired from the military in 2001 as a Chief Warrant Officer 2, after a career ending injury and is currently an advocate for women and disabled veterans. In 2011, Elizabeth received the Congressional Veteran Commendation from Senator Sam Johnson for her contributions to her community.

Elizabeth is a founding member of the John Maxwell Team of speakers, as well as an award-winning sales consultant.

A #1 Best Selling Author in *Succeeding in Spite of Everything*, Elizabeth is currently writing her biography, *Soaring Further*. Elizabeth lives in Dallas-Fort Worth.

**Elizabeth McCormick**
Email: elizabeth@yourinspirationalspeaker.com
Website: www.yourinspirationalspeaker.com

Follow Elizabeth:
Twitter: @elizabeth_helo
www.facebook.com/blackhawkpilot

# Fear Changed My Life

By Kelley Moore

*This story is dedicated to loud, boisterous, adventurous kids in cafegymatoriums around the world. It's time to SHOUT LOUD AND PROUD!*

*This story is dedicated to rebellious teenagers because I see you, and I totally get it.*

*This story is dedicated to my parents, JD and Ann, and my brother, Clay. I know life growing up with me was unpredictable, to say the least.*

*This story is dedicated to my beautiful daughters, Vicki and Rebecca, who inspire me daily to live boldly, love deeply and laugh loudly!*

*And, finally, this story is dedicated to my hottie hubby, Dale. Words are so inadequate to express the depth of my gratitude.*

*I love y'all!*

## Fall 1975

We gathered on the hard wood floor of the "cafegymatoruim"—that hybrid room that is a cross between a cafeteria, a gymnasium and an auditorium that one can find in thousands of elementary schools around the world. I was five and just one of the sixty or so kindergartners anxiously awaiting the "BIG" news the teachers had been teasing us with for days.

"We are putting on a play for the whole school, our families and the entire community," they announced, "and everyone will have a part to play."

There were some groans, some shouts of glee and lots of squirming, squiggling, and giggling as the teachers went around handing out the parts.

I was so excited! I loved to act! I loved to perform! In fact, I was a ringleader in many a classroom antic. I just knew I would be chosen first and given the leading role. I would be the super hero that would fly-in boldly and save the day! I would be the star of the show!! Ta-da!!!!

*"My debut performance and I'm only five;" "Fame, fortune, stardom are mine! I'll have fans everywhere and Hollywood will love me!"* were thoughts running through my over-active imagination. As you can imagine, I was a ball-of-fire sort of kid. I lived life full out every moment. I often wonder if I were a kid in today's environment if I'd be diagnosed with ADHD and drugged. I know I wore my poor folk's plum out and challenged many a teacher. I can imagine that my name is on 1000s of premature gray hairs! *(Gratitude and blessings to Mrs. Johnson & Wycoff & Swint & all the others—I really did try to "be good"!)*

Back in that cafegymatorium, the teachers handed out the speaking parts and then divided the rest of us—girls on one side and boys on the other. I was still trying to overcome the shock of not getting a speaking part and the death of my Hollywood dreams when the next words I heard froze time. All the rest of us girls would be flowers—delicate and graceful and quiet and still.

202

I am none of those things!

I am not delicate. I am not graceful. I am most certainly not quiet. And, still? I'm not even still when I sleep—even to this day!

Just as I began to sink deeper into the floor because I knew there was no way I wasn't going to be in big trouble during this whole "school play" experience—*in my mind I figured I'd probably end up kicked out of school for squirming and whispering jokes to the other flowers and end up homeless and broke for the rest of my life. I was a total failure already at five just because of who I was (or, err, wasn't)* —my teacher noticed my distress. She came over and placed her hands on my shoulders, looked into my teary, frightened eyes and said, "And you'll be our narrator, Kelley, because we know that *even without a microphone* you will be heard all the way to the very back."

"GASP!" What did she just say?!

My greatest nemesis, my loudness, had all of a sudden become my greatest asset. For my entire five long years of life, I'd gotten in trouble DAILY…almost minute-by-minute, for my loudness and now here I was being chosen to lead the play because of it. My Hollywood dreams weren't dead after all??

My voice, the very essence of me, was always getting me into trouble. I was too loud, talked too much, asked way too many questions, was too full of myself, too…too…too much. Yet, here I was being given the largest responsibility in the whole project simply because of my ability to be loud and clear.

Talk about confusing.

Oh, and something even more confusing, other people were mad! Some of the kids were really mad that I had the most words to say. Some kids didn't even get to say one word. I spoke in every scene.

Some kids decided to stop being my friend because I got that part. Some grownups were mad because—well, I really didn't know why they were mad, they just were and I knew about it and it scared me. I overheard things like, "She's just out for attention." "That sure is one arrogant, conceited kid." "Boy, what a loud mouth troublemaker." All because I had a loud voice and an outgoing, gregarious, fun-loving personality. I wasn't liked because of my voice and I couldn't control it. I decided my voice was dangerous and scary and that until I could become calm and soft-spoken I would be unworthy. From that moment on, I began a journey to be anything and anyone BUT my natural self. I began an internal battle that I still engage in today.

I made it through that play all those years ago (and yes, I was heard in the very back row without a microphone!) and then I began to ache. I began to ache because I loved the power of my voice. I loved using words and my voice and my enthusiasm to move an audience. I loved how powerful I felt and how commanding I could be. I loved that I could evoke emotion with words and the way I spoke them. Some people really loved me and showered me with attention and praise and I felt so good and happy. But other people were mean and for some reason I could only hear the hate, so I began to hate. I learned to dread the sound of my own voice, while also loving the power of my voice. I began to hate my desire to lead and instigate fun and push limits and live big. I had no idea how to use the gifts I'd been given to support others instead of frightening them. I was five years old.

How was I to know when to speak out and when to hold back?

How was I to become quiet and calm and soft-spoken when my exuberance and passion and zest literally exploded out of me?

I learned…

...If I'm loud and boisterous and "out there", some won't like me and they'll leave me out...

...I'm invisible.

I learned...

...If I'm quiet and shrink and hold back, then I don't get noticed at all...

...I'm invisible.

I began to ache because I knew I had to hide all the things I loved because **other people** got hurt because I loved those things and I was good at them. I didn't understand it. I just knew it was true.

Talk about confusing.

Fast-forward eight years...

**Fall 1983**

The lights were low, the crowd was ready, I heard my name announced.

I walked out onto the huge stage and faced thousands of strangers. I picked up the microphone and opened my mouth. Five minutes later, the crowd erupted in applause, love pouring forth from the audience. I had done it! I had just won the talent portion of Ms. Teen Texas by giving a speech...by using my powerful voice to convey a message of faith, trust, and hope.

I loved it! I loved the whole process of exploring what I thought about an issue—this particular topic was my generation and the war on drugs—and then communicating those thoughts in such a way that they moved others. I loved dreaming about speaking up for my peers and reminding the world that we are courageous and committed to a world that is open and accepting for all. I loved freely expressing myself.

And then, fear spoke up. The judges called me "the voice of her generation."

That's a lot of responsibility. What if I say the wrong thing? What if my words cause damage? What gives me the right to speak for others?

I was terrified.

How could I be the "voice of a generation?" I'm just a silly little girl from South Texas that continually gets in trouble for talking too much; for being too loud; for being too…too…too much yet never enough—never good enough, never pretty enough, never quiet enough…I vowed in that moment to never raise my voice to a crowd again—it's too much.

I began to ache because I knew I had to hide all the things I loved because **I** could get hurt because I loved those things and was good at them. I didn't understand it. I just knew it was true.

Talk about confusing.

Fast-forward a few months…

## High School

I used my voice and my over-the-top antics to my advantage in the social scene. Kids loved it when I boldly called out the teachers and used sarcasm and wit to push the envelope. Teachers didn't love it so much.

Boys loved it when I said yes, even though deep inside I really meant no. I was afraid they wouldn't like me or I'd be left out of the fun that turned out to really not be all that fun. I found myself in situations where I needed to speak up for myself and instead I sacrificed the very core of me when I didn't.

I ended up becoming a master chameleon and a master manipulator—I wish I could report that I only manipulated my own feelings and desires and truths, but I have to face the cold fact that I used my voice and words like a weapon a lot. Oh, and boy could I lie like nobody's business; I even passed a lie detector test to get a job when I was 15 and couldn't legally have the sales job I got until I was 16 so I changed my birth year on documents, went to the police station, got hooked up to a machine, looked a Detective square in the face and lied blatantly. Sure, I was scared, but I had long ago figured out how to calm my physical reactions to fear and threats. I had become numb to my own pain and therefore numb to any pain I might cause others. There were some days that I sold enough to make over $20 an hour as a fifteen year old! My ability to string together words and phrases and deliver them in such a way as to emotionally touch people made my sales skyrocket! I was dangerous.

I pushed all the envelopes, limits, and boundaries I could in an effort to get attention. Sometimes I was able to channel my energies and abilities for good, but mostly I lived for drama.

My actions and choices were full of cries to notice ME—the real me that I had become a master at hiding. My actions and choices were designed by me to help me fit in and feel better when what really happened was I felt invisible, misunderstood, and left out. I was consumed with ME. ME. ME. ME.

I ended up losing everything I had ever deep down inside really wanted:

1. I mouthed off to my coaches so I got kicked off the team.
2. I mouthed off to my teachers so I failed.
3. I mouthed off to my parents and damaged the only people that truly loved the "real" me.

All that mouthing off resulted in severe consequences. I failed high school! I would not be allowed to graduate with my class. I learned this news only days before the ceremony. Invitations to parties were in the hands of 100s of people. Plans were in motion. Venues booked. Food cooked. I had received gifts. Relatives were already en route from far and wide to celebrate and honor me. My parents were devastated. I was pretty sure I had lost everything. I was a total flame out at seventeen. The damage to those I loved and cared about was deep. The damage to myself was almost fatal.

I had lost my self-respect, my dignity, and my trust in myself. What a joke to think I would ever fit in anywhere—I didn't fit in with ME. I was so consumed with ME, yet I didn't even really know me, nor did I care enough about me to get to know me. I was my biggest enemy yet I blamed others for making my life suck. They forced me to misbehave. It's their fault I'm a failure. I was a victim and life wasn't fair.

I just wanted it all to be over, so I gathered close to 100 aspirin and I took every one of them.

The moment I swallowed, something inside of me started screaming that I was wrong; that I could be more. That I had gifts to share and good work to do in the world and that I needed to change something. I needed to change myself. I ran across the street to my neighbor and told her what I did. I begged her to keep my secret and to keep me alive! She did both! She knew I didn't really want to die. She knew I didn't have any deep-seated psychological illness. She knew I just needed to be seen and heard and a chance. She braided my hair, talked to me, held me, encouraged me and loved me. She gave me hope. She dared me to ask different questions about where I found myself and how I felt. She challenged me to fight for myself. She kept me awake and she awakened me. I owe her my life.

The next day, I reached deep inside and I begged and pleaded the school administration and convinced them to let me take a correspondence course instead of having to repeat my entire senior year. I promised I would do something big with my life. I promised I would change. I promised I would make better decisions and choices if they just gave me a chance. By grace, they said yes, so I took a mail order course in kinesiology, passed it and received my Advanced Academic with Honors Diploma 20 days after everyone else in my class.

What had my mouth gotten me into now? I'd never really kept a promise before, but this time I knew something had to be different...

Talk about confusing.

Fast-forward just a couple of days...

## June 1988

The night is dark; a deep, bone-chilling darkness without a single star, no moonlight, no lights outside the windows. It's June 21, 1988, somewhere around 2:30 AM and I've been traveling since noon the day before. I've been on 'em all: planes, trains, automobiles—and now a bus—a BIG bus. The biggest bus I've ever seen in my short seventeen years of life. I'm alone.

The bus glides to a stop; the airbrakes "hisssssss;" then silence; a silence so profound I can actually feel it. The only sound I hear is the sound of my heartbeat and the heartbeats of the other souls on the bus with me. I finally acknowledge the FEAR.

*"What am I doing here? Do I have what it takes? I have never really tried to do anything that I didn't know FOR SURE I would be good at or could try to talk my way out of. What have I done? I can't mouth off and get myself outta this one without going to prison!" I thought*

*the voice in my head was loud until I heard,* **"GET OFF MY BUS! GET OFF MY STINKIN' BUS AND GET ON MY YELLOW FOOTPRINTS—NOW!!"**

I had arrived at Marine Corps Boot Camp, Parris Island, South Carolina.

This was the "something big" I decided to do with my life. I wanted to push the farthest limit I could imagine. I wanted to go for something that no one thought I could do. I wanted to prove to myself and to everyone else that I could.

Let me tell you, in that moment (and plenty of other moments throughout the course of boot camp!) my heart pounded with fear.

### Fear changed my life.

I was afraid I had made a huge mistake. I was afraid I couldn't handle the challenges I faced. I was afraid to make the drill instructor mad. I was afraid I wouldn't be good enough.

I was afraid of my thoughts, so I *quit thinking* and did what I was told to do. I got off the bus.

When I heard that first unforgettable bellow, I heard that voice in my head asking again, ***"What are you doing here? You have never really achieved anything in your entire life. You hide and pretend. You are a fraud not a warrior. You are a failure. You are arrogant, conceited, and a loudmouth—everyone says so. Everyone is laughing at you—again! And this time when you flame out, you'll bring shame not only to yourself, but also to your dad and your uncles that did earn the title. No one believes you can do this. What have you done?"***

As I stood virtually paralyzed on those footprints, I started listening to the loud, clear, direct voices that guided me. That voice that continued

210

to roar orders at me was commanding. It got my attention. It was clear. It was decisive. It was the voice of a leader. As strange as it was in that moment, I realized that the strength of that voice helped me feel safe. Could I use MY voice that way?

Fast-forward 25 years…

I did graduate boot camp. In fact, I was the guide of my platoon from training day one and graduated at the top of my series. I achieved the rank of non-commissioned officer, traveled around the world, and developed leadership traits that allow me to accomplish any mission I choose.

Looking back, I can clearly see that I was on a very unique training path created especially for me so that I could teach others how to find their voice and live their own version of life full out.

I learned how to remove the armor of bravado protecting that loud, boisterous five year old and choose instead to be courageous and show up as fully me—loud, inquisitive, silly, and sassy me. I learned to remove the cloak of cockiness from teenage Kelley and embrace instead the quiet confidence that comes from knowing I am doing the best I can with what I've got in each moment and so is every other human soul.

And, most importantly, I learned how to love myself and once I could do that, I found the love of my life. I married a fellow Marine and now decades later we have two amazing daughters that absolutely embrace their power and raise their voices.

And I learned that it is my life's mission to awaken courage, confidence and commitment within every human. When hard times hit us, it's not easy to see a way out. When life overwhelms us, it's human nature to rage and question and grieve. I know so much about courage because I am wickedly intimate with fear. I understand at a gut level about confidence because doubt is one of my constant companions. I truly get what commitment is because apathy and indifference latch onto me with a vengeance. It's a daily practice for me to choose courage. It's a moment-by-moment choice to face my doubts and act "as if" until I can really believe. It's a visceral exercise with each breath to stay the course and keep the faith. If this silly little girl from South Texas who can't even pass high school can do it, so can you!

Choose COURAGE. Embrace CONFIDENCE.
Make a COMMITMENT.

Do-Over
By: Kelley Moore

Late at night, when all alone, with the thoughts deep in your head;
Do you think on happiness, laughter and joy?
Or do you dwell on thoughts of dread?

Does the sound of your voice as you spoke through the day
Bring a smile upon your face?
Or were the words that you spoke meant to harm others
Instead of words of kindness, acceptance, and grace?

As you look back upon your actions and choices,
Were they honorable and true?
Or in those late night thoughts in your head,
Do you wish for a "Do-Over" or two?

Good news my friends stuck in that land of dread
Longing for just one more shot.
As long as you're having those thoughts in your head
Finished…it is NOT!

Tomorrow will come with its good and its bad
And many choices you must face.
You can choose once again to speak harshly.
Or to speak words of kindness and grace.

Each day is a chance for that "Do-Over"
You get to do it all again.
You get to rejoice in all our differences; to listen;
To learn…to be a friend.

Kelley Moore, America's Courage Coach

The University of Illinois calls Kelley a "powerful relationship strategist." She calls herself a "Marine in Mom's clothes."

Kelley began her career in service to others by serving our country as a member of our nation's most elite fighting force, the United States Marine Corps, where she developed the values necessary to succeed in any environment and began to truly believe that each of us possesses a deep, internal wisdom that allows us to access the resources we need at exactly the right time to achieve whatever mission we choose.

Kelley has the ability to speak the language of every person in an organization, from the CEO to the front-line "troops." A former non-profit executive, an award-winning sales and marketing consultant, a business owner, a Professional Behaviors and Values Analyst, and a Mom to two active and creative girls, Kelley brings a blend of education, insight, sound principles, and FUN that is crucial to success.

As America's Courage Coach, Kelley works with organizations and their members to recognize, accept and develop their inherent potential and see their unique possibilities. From young to old, Kelley speaks the language of courage, confidence and commitment. It is never too early and never too late to live the life you desire. The choice is truly yours!

**Kelley Moore**
Email: kmoore@seeyourpossibilities.com
Website: www.SeeYourPossibilities.com

Follow Kelley:
Facebook: https://www.facebook.com/kelley.u.moore
Twitter: https://twitter.com/KelleyMoore

# POWER OF INSPIRATION

# Just Plain and Simple Faith

### By Stu Schlackman

*This chapter is dedicated to all of you who are seeking the truth. I believe the truth is right in front of us as God intended through his son Jesus Christ or as it is said in Hebrew-Yeshua the Messiah. He has been promised to us in the Old Testament throughout all its books describing who he is and what he would do. Please know there is more than this life. It says in Ecclesiastes 3:11: "He has made everything beautiful in its time. He has also set eternity in the hearts of men; yet they cannot fathom what God has done from beginning to end".*

*God has created all of us for his purpose. Please know that I have explored the Scriptures and truly believe we will know the truth by Faith in God's promise to us – His Son.*

In 1983 I moved from Nashua, New Hampshire to Birmingham, Alabama as I transitioned into the world of sales. As a nice Jewish boy from New York City I was now living in the *Bible Belt*. When my new sales manager Bob Baines welcomed me to his sales team, I had no idea that the career transition would also transform my spiritual life. But it most definitely did. Here's how the 'domino effect' went to work – in a very good way.

On a business trip to Knoxville, Tennessee accompanied by my boss, Bob, I was introduced to Greg Christian. One night over Mexican food (fairly foreign to me at the time), the three of us had the most fascinating conversation I've had to date. While our initial small talk revolved around my assessment of chips and salsa in the North versus the South, the dialogue soon turned spiritual.

In the course of my first few bites, Greg hit me with, "So, what do you think of sin?

I came back with, "What do you mean?"

"Stu, I mean have you been forgiven for your sins?"

"Maybe Bob told you, I'm Jewish. Well, as one of the chosen people any sins were forgiven because I have fasted on Yom Kippur." I didn't take a proud tone; I was merely explaining the facts as I knew them to be. Greg respectfully gave me his full attention while I spoke. And he took pause to think before he voiced his thoughts.

"That's around this time of year, right, in the fall? You must have just fasted then." I could have made a general comment to concur that Yom Kippur was indeed in autumn. I could have reacted as if it (the part about me having just fasted) weren't a question. Technically, it wasn't worded as a question. But, I knew he was looking for confirmation.

I fessed up. "Well, no, not this year." I covered my disobedience with, "But, I often do." I went on. "Sin is what separates us from God, I know, but we are reconciled from our sins when we fast on Yom Kippur to repent. Plus, when we do good works and help others God is pleased."

Greg delicately, yet convincingly, illustrated how I had touched on an important fact when I mentioned that sin separated us from God. He boiled it all back down to the fall of Adam and Eve in the Garden of Eden when Eve let Satan (or the "serpent" as Greg also referred to him) convince her to take a bite of the apple from the Tree of Knowledge of

Good and Evil and in so doing went against God's commandment. "Sin," he stressed, "equates to death. Because Adam and Eve sinned in the garden, they would not be able to live forever. Ever since, there has been a battle going on between good and evil (God and Satan)."

I interjected. "But how does that relate to us today, here and now?"

"Well, because they fell for Satan's ploy, we've all been in a mess ever since. Think about it. I mean when you look at the world around you, you see what's going on. We're in a big pickle." This wasn't too hard for me to believe. The world had then a host of problems and it still does – war, drugs, disease, and corruption. I had always believed in God's creation and good and evil. It dawned on me that as mankind evolved and developed more intelligence, people would surely want to control and diminish evil. But such is not nearly the case.

I was following Greg, and so he didn't stop there. He jumped ahead, in an effort to connect it all for me. "Jesus came later – as God's son – to reconcile everyone back to God, by dying on the cross for our sins. To take on the sins of the world, for all of mankind. You and everyone else have the opportunity to accept Him as our Lord and Savior."

*That includes me*, I thought. But, God couldn't possibly have had a son. The thought of Jesus Christ transported me back to my initial encounter with the awareness of His existence – to the dinner table at Tommy McGrath's apartment, complete with baked ham. I recalled how upon my return home Mom had looked horrified at the mere mention of the name of Jesus. Donning a crisp tone, she disputed the information I spewed out and abruptly put the topic – and me – to bed. Here was Greg bringing it to the table again.

Another bite of my enchilada and I subsequently spoke up, "Other than God and his angels, and his creation of men and women, I was taught there's nothing in between God and man. It's not possible for God to have a son."

Greg disputed that, in a very polite manner, by sharing with me about Mary and what he termed "the virgin birth." He excitedly went on saying, "Jesus descended through the lineage of your Abraham, Stu. You know about Judah, one of Jacob's sons. Jesus was a direct descendent. And in *Genesis 49*, verse 10, it says: 'The scepter will not depart from Judah, ...' That means the Messiah would eventually come from Judah, which is what happened. Jesus is that Messiah, the Savior of our world. You did grow up with the belief in God's word that there would be a Messiah, didn't you?" I answered as best I could. "I grew up with some vague understanding of a Messiah."

Greg was ready with more explanation. "You see, what happened was that when Jesus died on the cross there were Jewish people who believed in Him and accepted Him as their Messiah and others who rejected Him. The ones who rejected Him did so because they saw Him as a threat to all Jewish people and a threat to their position and status under Roman rule." I remember that I couldn't help but think and admire how well Greg knew his stuff. He didn't have a Bible in tow, but he assuredly quoted Scripture.

That very night, Greg briefly ran down the entire Bible from *Genesis* to *Revelation* (of which I knew nothing, as I knew nothing of the New Testament, period). All the while, his level of enthusiasm – as well as Bob's – never waned, as they both shared their faith. They obviously didn't bother with concern over me rejecting their beliefs as the Jews long ago had rejected Jesus.

Even as Greg mentioned the miracles and healings Jesus performed throughout the four gospels – the books of *Matthew, Mark, Luke* and *John* – I listened with an open mind. I certainly didn't possess the knowledge to intelligently dispute anything he was saying about the spread of Christianity.  Plus, I was fascinated.  The bottom line to what Greg was talking about is a hope in the future of the return of Jesus and the promise of eternity in heaven with God!  His voice almost sang when he said, "From Genesis to Revelation, God has laid out His plan of salvation to bring His creation back to Him.  We know Jesus will return to save the world."

There was much to mull over on the way back to my hotel and once I reached my room.  My mind was racing back and forth from what I had always been told regarding religion and what Greg had to say about God.  I pondered my heritage:  Judaism looked backward – through traditions based on what had already taken place.  All the holidays we celebrated were reminders and reenactments of what our people had gone through in the past – the suffering in Egypt, almost being obliterated by Haman during Purim, and the survival of Judas and the Maccabees during Hanukkah.

There's a joke that sums up the entire history of the Jewish people in nine words: *They tried to kill us, we won, let's eat.*  There's frequently a little (or a lot of) truth to jokes and it is such forward honesty that brings us to hearty laughter.

*What if I were to believe in this person of Jesus as the true Messiah? Did He really die on the cross and rise from the dead?  For our sins? And would belief in Him as my Lord and Savior truly free me from sin – for eternity?  And would it then keep me from being separated from God?  But, would I be rejected by my family and friends if I believed all this?*  I had heard that long ago some Orthodox Jewish families would renounce their family members who believed in Him as the Messiah. **Oy Veh!**  And, supposedly, they went to the extreme of holding mock burials for those believers.  **Oy oy veh!!**

*So, if I accept Jesus as my Lord and Savior, what would it say about my conviction in being Jewish?*  All I heard that night went against what I

221

had been brought up to believe via Grandpa, my parents, and my Jewish studies. Yet, with a forthcoming nature Greg fervently shared the gospel as he knew it, and not for a moment did I believe he was trying to sell me. There was no commission to be earned. He seemed genuinely concerned that I did not believe in the person of Jesus; he appeared to sincerely care about my salvation. On top of being well-informed, he was enormously passionate about his beliefs. To be painfully honest, both Greg's and Bob's demeanors were far cries from the "radical rabbi" comments my own dear mother had vehemently made when I even brought up the name "Jesus."

****

A few days passed, and I hadn't been able to cease contemplating that dinner discussion. Back in Birmingham, Bob invited me to his church – a Baptist church. He picked me up early in order to make it in time for the Sunday school class. It was my first Bible class since the days in Hebrew school, yet I was familiar to a degree with the lesson – on *Second Kings*. The teacher brought up the Jewish people, and I nervously whispered a troubled comment or two to Bob. The teacher noticed us chatting and asked if we had any questions.

"Tell him," urged Bob.

"Tell him what?" I asked.

"Go ahead, Stu. Tell him you're Jewish."

And so I took his cue. And you would have thought a celebrity the likes of Steven Spielberg had entered the room. No, just Stu Schlackman. My last name often gave away my heritage, but this time it was the public declaration of my Judaism. My nervousness faded quickly.

To say I wasn't used to openly talking about my Judaism is a colossal understatement. I almost never brought it up unless questioned about it. Where I came from, it seemed that the topic of religion or any spiritual discussion stayed undercover, deemed controversial and off limits as if it were secret CIA stuff. Conversely, in the South, I soon found that people in plain sight prayed over meals, met in public places for Bible studies, and overtly spoke of their faith.

*What is a good, Jewish boy from 'The Big Apple' supposed to do with this new information and radically different point of view about life and death?* I spent a tremendous amount of time deliberating. Over and over again, I questioned whether they had it right or I did. *Or, could two extremely different belief systems both be right?*

****

My head was spinning in a state of confusion. I was living by myself in a small hotel room until our new home was ready for us to move into and most nights I stuck to the routine of watching a television program or two before going to sleep. One night, I got a different urge. Or – better yet – God had other plans for me.

As I curiously opened the drawer to the nightstand, a Gideon's Bible stared up at me. I pulled it out of hiding. I thumbed through books I recognized – *Genesis, Exodus, Judges, Samuel* ... As I made my way along, I noticed books with the names *Hosea* and *Joel* and others that I had pretty much forgotten about. Finally, after seeing *Malachi*, the next page appeared to me as a giant billboard in the sky flashing the words *The New Testament (The Gospel of Jesus Christ).*

Shock set in rapidly. I gave myself some attitude as aloud I said, "What in the world is this stuff doing in the Bible?!" Insult and invasion (into my Holy Scriptures) joined the shock. Sure, Greg had conveyed the story of the entire Bible to me, but I hadn't realized until my quick trip through Gideon that the Bible that Greg spoke of included both testaments. I was appalled, but not too appalled to dig in and check it out more thoroughly. This was considerably better than any TV drama. I noticed the books of *Matthew, Mark, Romans* ... and I finally got to one I supposed was kosher (used in slang as *okay* or *acceptable*) – *Hebrews*. I wondered, *Can this all be true?* I had no answers. The hotel walls had no answers. Within a few minutes, with the Bible in my hands, an answer came in the form of a question. A voice in my head clearly argued, *Are you calling me a liar?* Why would I say that to myself? It had to have been from another source – maybe the whisper of God. Who is in control of our thoughts – us or God?

I was always rational, so the only way I knew to approach this conundrum was from a logical perspective. To sort it all out, I started by asking more questions of myself and the universe: *Why would one part (Old Testament) of the Bible be true and the next part (New Testament) be false? Why were both books bound together if only one was valid? Who am I to say that only my half was true and the New Testament was not true? What evidence do I possess to disprove the New Testament?*

While its foundation is in Judaism, Christians believe in the Old Testament. Christians and Jews alike believe that Jesus was a rabbi who came from the Jewish faith. Logic told me that I would either have to negate the entire Bible or believe in the entire Bible, and I couldn't deny the Old Testament – so I needed to not reject the New Testament. This seemed simple enough. But, there is a big difference between *not rejecting* and *accepting. Many people have accepted Jesus as the Messiah. Why?* No one had ever given me solid reasoning why not to believe – they just told me not to believe. Those extremely bright people who directed me not to believe required more proof to believe and discounted anything they couldn't see.

With the judicial system we are innocent until proven guilty, not the other way around. Perhaps, over-thinking things when it comes to faith verges on an oxymoron. My faith at a standstill for the time at hand, I was left with the reality that I needed to further explore the New Testament and at least learn more about the person of Jesus Christ. In the following days, I did just that.

**** 

Once my family had returned from Houston and the three of us settled into our new house, I took the time to revisit Shades Mountain Baptist Church, with Bob. It was the Sunday before Christmas. To my surprise, Bob had set up a meeting with Dr. Charles T. Carter, the pastor. After the church service, Bob and I sat down with Dr. Carter. Twenty minutes into the conversation, the pastor asked if I believed that Jesus was the Son of God. It took 30 seconds of forethought to find my reply, but then with more than a mutter I clearly said, "I think so."

I had found no real reason to reject Him since I had come to discover – and believe (through my exploration I found no reason to disbelieve) – in the writings of the New Testament. I did believe in Him as God's Son, but I wasn't sure what to think beyond that or what to do about it. Since I told Dr. Carter that I did believe in Jesus as God's Son, he said he wanted to help me out with the "next step." He asked me to come back the following Sunday to "be baptized in front of the congregation" and place membership with them. I told him that I'd have to get back with him.

I wasn't in the door more than a few minutes before I shared my experience with my wife. Her response: "No way." Those two words were her way of letting me know she did not want us to join a Baptist church. The search began for a Church of Christ. Without many in our immediate vicinity, it didn't take long before we struck gold and agreed on Hoover Church of Christ. The minister was 28-year-old Gary Bradley, Jr. A graduate of David Lipscomb University, he was a rather impressive speaker. Until then, I hadn't realized Bible colleges existed, but I wasn't too taken by surprise since I knew of Yeshiva University (a university in New York City for Jewish studies).

****

Complete shock came one Monday evening – after having attended church on Sunday at Hoover – when the doorbell rang and Pastor Gary and one of the deacons from the church, Jim Gregory, stood at our door. This was a first. No one ever just popped on over, with the exception of during my childhood when my neighborhood pals came calling. Regardless, I wasn't put off whatsoever. Gary and Jim kindly asked if they could spend about 30 minutes visiting. I cordially agreed, because I was curious. And for the next half hour or so they led a Bible study of sorts in my living room. No biggie. Good stuff.

Before leaving, Gary forged ahead by asking if they could make a return visit or two. Turning him down was out of the question. He and Jim had given me their precious time, their undivided attention. I responded with a nod and, "Yeah, sure."

They visited us in our home a total of three times. Each time they reminded me of the issue of "sin." It was as if they took over where the dinner conversation with Bob and Greg had left off a month earlier. "Jesus was the perfect sacrifice for us all," Gary said on more than one occasion.

I definitely agreed, aware that in the Old Testament within *Leviticus* priests sacrificed animals to God in order to cover the sins of the people.

On the initial visit, before I could even breathe a word about the fasting we Jews did on Yom Kippur to be forgiven for our sins, Gary was

226

ready for me. I'm not sure how he knew. "The holiday of Yom Kippur cannot permanently forgive your sins. It literally just rolls your sins forward until the next year at Yom Kippur."

Gary and Jim shared with me the Scripture from *Hebrews 10:11-14*: "Day after day every priest stands and performs his religious duties; again and again he offers the same sacrifices, which can never take away sins. But when this priest had offered for all time one sacrifice for sins, he sat down at the right hand of God. Since that time he waits for his enemies to be made his footstool, because by one sacrifice he has made perfect forever those who are being made holy."

Gary added, "The point, Stu, is that unlike fasting on Yom Kippur, the sacrifice of Jesus took care of sin once and for all – for the past, the present, the future. In *Hebrews*, chapter 9, in verse 22, it says, 'In fact, the law requires that nearly everything be cleansed with blood, and without the shedding of blood there is no forgiveness.'"

Jim clarified, "Jesus was the ultimate sacrifice shedding His own blood for forgiveness of our sins. His blood was what did away with our sins."

Despite the annual fasting on Yom Kippur being ingrained in me, it did seem unreasonable to have to cleanse the slate each year. Still, I brought it up again.

With that, Greg quoted *Hebrews*, chapter 10, again. This time, verse 3: "But those sacrifices are an annual reminder of sins, because it is impossible for the blood of bulls and goats to take away sins."

This spoke loudly to me. As long as I had been a quasi-practicing Jew, I had never witnessed a bull or goat being sacrificed. I wondered why – I thought we had to follow the Jewish laws as they were stated. *Why was the sacrificial system eventually abolished?* I questioned it then, but I know the answer now: when in captivity, despite their good intentions the Jewish people were not able to follow the sacrificial system that God had put in place in *Leviticus*. But, with Israel now a free state, they certainly had the ability to restore into play what God had commanded of them. Ah, but from what I understood growing up, prayer and doing good deeds – mitzvahs – had taken the place of sacrifice.

Seeing that I was beginning to grasp the issue of sin, and the concept of Jesus as the ultimate sacrifice, on the second visit Gary and Jim wanted to make sure I knew the coming of Jesus hadn't come out of the blue. "His birth was prophesized in the Old Testament," Gary said. "In *Deuteronomy*, chapter 18, verse 15: 'The LORD your God will raise up for you a prophet like me from among your own brothers. You must listen to him.' And verse 18, the words of Moses to the Children of Israel: 'I will raise up for them a prophet like you from among their brothers; I will put my words in his mouth, and he will tell them everything I command him.'"

Okay, so there would be a prophet. *Was that prophet really Jesus?* It crossed my mind that maybe it was someone else, as the Scripture from *Deuteronomy* seemed vague. It wasn't as convincing as other Scriptures they shared – that is until they got down to the business of presenting me with more Scriptures on the prophecies in the Old Testament and the fulfillment of those prophecies in the New Testament:

OLD TESTAMENT PROPHECY:
*Psalm 2:7*: "I will proclaim the decree of the Lord: He said to me, 'You are my Son; today I have become your Father.'"

It certainly seemed that God was talking about having a Son.

NEW TESTAMENT FULFILLMENT:

*Matthew 3:17*: "And a voice from heaven said, 'This is my Son, whom I love; with Him I am well pleased.'"

Any voice from heaven had to be God.

OLD TESTAMENT PROPHECY:
*Micah 5:2*: "'But you, Bethlehem Ephrathah, though you are small among the clans of Judah, out of you will come for me one who will be ruler over Israel, whose origins are from old, from ancient times.'"

NEW TESTAMENT FULFILLMENT:
*Matthew 2:1*: "After Jesus was born in Bethlehem in Judea, during the time of King Herod …"

So far, this all seemed beyond coincidence.

OLD TESTAMENT PROPHECY:
*Isaiah 7:14*: "Therefore the Lord himself will give you a sign: The virgin will be with child and will give birth to a son and will call him Immanuel."

Upon hearing this very specific prophecy, an analogy came to mind. It's kind of like saying that in 1952 a kid will be born in Bronx, New York, his name will be Stuart Schlackman, and he will weigh 6 pounds 15 ounces. Sure enough, here I am in the flesh.

NEW TESTAMENT FULFILLMENT:
*Matthew 1:23*: "The virgin will be with child and will give birth to a son, and they will call him Immanuel – which means, 'God with us.'"

OLD TESTAMENT PROPHECY:
*Psalm 2:6*: "I have installed my King on Zion, my holy hill."

*Isaiah 59:20*: "'The Redeemer will come to Zion, to those in Jacob who repent of their sins,' declares the LORD."

*Micah 4:2*: "...The law will go out from Zion, the word of the LORD from Jerusalem."

For a short time, I was slightly confused. Growing up I was told that Moses was given the law (commandments) on Mount Sinai. Gary and Jim were focusing on Zion when it came to God's King. Gary taught me that Zion was a hill right outside the walls of the old city of Jerusalem. Zion became a synecdoche referring to the entire city of Jerusalem in the Land of Israel.

NEW TESTAMENT FULFILLMENT:
*Matthew 27:37*: "Above his head they placed the written charge against Him: THIS IS JESUS, THE KING OF THE JEWS."

Now I saw that Jim and Gary were referencing to Jesus as King of the Jews.

For the most part, I was still following my guests. They went deeper. The prophecies didn't end there. They gave me more:

OLD TESTAMENT PROPHECY:
*Zechariah 9:9*: "Rejoice greatly O daughter of Zion! Shout, Daughter of Jerusalem! See, your king comes to you, righteous and having salvation, gentle and riding on a donkey, on a colt, the foal of a donkey."

NEW TESTAMENT FULFILLMENT:
*Luke 19:35-36*: "They brought it to Jesus, threw their cloaks on the colt and put Jesus on it. As he went along, people spread their cloaks on the road."

## OLD TESTAMENT PROPHECY:

*Zechariah 11:12:* "I told them, 'If you think it best, give me my pay; but if not, keep it.' So they paid me thirty pieces of silver."

Okay, someone was paid 30 pieces of silver for a job well done. But, they validated it. This was getting more interesting by the minute.

## NEW TESTAMENT FULFILLMENT:

*Matthew 26:14-15:* "then one of the Twelve – the one called Judas Iscariot – went to the chief priests and asked, 'What are you willing to give me if I hand him over to you?' So they counted out for him thirty silver coins."

Indeed, Judas Iscariot, one of Jesus' disciples, betrayed him for those 30 pieces of silver.

As Gary and Jim sat in my living room quoting the Bible, I determined that the Scriptures in fact gave new meaning to the word 'coincidence.' Their much appreciated visit began to wind down with verses from *Psalms* and *Luke*:

## OLD TESTAMENT PROPHECY:

*Psalm 22:16:* "Dogs have surrounded me; a band of evil men has encircled me, they have pierced my hands and feet."

Clearly, someone was being tortured. Additionally, in verse 18, it's written that his garments were to be divided and cast into lots. At the time when the *Psalms* were written (1000 years before Jesus), crucifixion did not yet exist. *How could the writer have been so descriptive about something he did not know about?* My mind went to an analogy again: In 1885, I couldn't have described the shape and size of a vehicle that would later be used for travel to the moon! It wasn't even fathomable, but it happened in 1969.

NEW TESTAMENT FULFILLMENT:
*Luke 23:33-34*: "When they came to the place called the Skull, there they crucified him, along with the criminals, one on his right, the other on his left. Jesus said, 'Father, forgive them, for they do not know what they are doing.' And they divided up his clothes by casting lots."

Crucifixion was used by the Romans as the most despicable, cruel and insulting way of death for a thief. This is how God chose to have His Son die as the ultimate sacrifice for our sins. Jesus wasn't a thief. He was a rabbi of the Jewish people. Yet, the form of death for someone who wasn't with absolute certainty convicted of wrongdoings ends up being crucifixion! According to the Old Testament, the form of execution used back then was stoning per Jewish law. But with the Romans in control, crucifixion was the method of execution.

During our third time together, my two guests mainly focused on the entire chapter of *Isaiah 53* – which in the Old Testament goes into detail about a "man of sorrow" who was familiar with suffering. He was someone who was despised and rejected by men. He took up our infirmities and was crushed for our iniquities (our sins). He was pierced for our transgressions ("crucified and pierced in His side"). The Lord had put on Him the iniquities of us all. Again, He bore our sin. He was led like a lamb to the slaughter and did not open His mouth. The Lord made His life a guilt offering (to alleviate sin), and after the suffering of His soul He would "see the light of life" and be satisfied (raised from the dead). The last verse of the chapter says that He bore the sins of many and made intercession for the transgressors. From what they told me, I gathered that Jesus was the mediator for everyone's sins.

\*\*\*\*

Whew. That was a tremendous amount of material I was left with to regard. But because my education in sin and other biblical subject matter had begun even before I set foot in Alabama, it wasn't beyond my grasp. I put my own reason to work. I can well imagine that you, too, may be as baffled by all this as I once was. Truth is known to often baffle more than fiction. But, I got it – finally. Let me summarize what I gleaned from the Scriptures that I had been presented:

The Old Testament prophesizes that a woman, who is a virgin, will have a son in Bethlehem and he will become the ruler of Israel. This ruler will be called King of the Jews. He'll ride into town on a donkey. He'll be betrayed for thirty silver coins, and he'll be crucified (even though when it was prophesized crucifixion didn't yet exist).

What are the odds? What are the odds that even one person can predict that to happen? Slimmer than slim. Moreover, take into account that all those Old Testament prophecies were written at different times in history by different men. How is that possible? Yet, according to the Bible, every single one of those predictions was fulfilled.

When we compare it to a modern day analogy, well, it's not possible. Let's say that today in 2010 I predict that on March 18, 2084 a baby girl will be born in an elevator in Dallas, Texas, at 9:34 a.m. Two years from now, another person predicts the same baby will be named Isabel and she will weigh 8.7 pounds. In the year 2020, another person predicts that at age 18 the girl named Isabel will weigh 117 pounds and have a high school grade point average of 3.92. In 2040, someone else predicts that Isabel will be accepted to six universities and accept the invitation to the University of Texas. In 2058, another person predicts that Isabel will go to work for Texas Instruments in the accounting department and drive a car that flies made by Ford. Yet another person then predicts that Isabel at age 25 will marry her high school sweetheart and have two children. And then in 2066, another person predicts Isabel's accidental death in a bungee cord accident on the moon in the year 2179. Oh, and let me throw in that three days later it will be a miracle when Isabel, whose mother – by the way – conceived her despite never having had a sexual relationship, comes back to life.

Like I said – impossible.

*2 Peter 1:20-21* speaks for itself: "Above all, you must understand that no prophecy of Scripture came about by the prophet's own interpretation. For prophecy never had its origin in the will of man, but men spoke from God as they were carried along by the Holy Spirit."

Nothing, however, is impossible for God. What I've shared here represents only a few of the prophecies. There are some 300 prophecies in the Old Testament pointing to the coming of the Messiah.

There are probably happenings in your own life that you never could have – would have – predicted. If anyone had told me before the spring of 1983 that a few months later I would be living in Birmingham, Alabama and would become a Christian, I would have deemed that person nuts and the idea ludicrous. Yet, it came to be.

I recognize the uncertainty that forms for people, keeping them at arm's length when it comes to belief in the Bible – in God and His Son. But, there's no renouncing what the Holy Scriptures say, and there is no other book that speaks of God's plan for mankind's salvation. Once I realized this, I had one of three choices: 1) acknowledgement with acceptance as the truth, 2) acknowledgement with indifference, or 3) rejection.

I moved from a 3 to a 2 and on to a 1. I had enough substantiation. I now had faith that the person of Jesus (*Yeshua) was the chosen Messiah and God's Son who died for our sins.

****

On Wednesday night, February 22, 1984, at 31 years of age, I walked forward in the Hoover Church of Christ to accept Jesus as my Lord and Savior and was baptized by Pastor Gary Bradley, Jr.

Stu has spent over 25 years in sales management, sales and sales training with world class companies like Digital Equipment Corporation, Cap Gemini and EDS. His focus is on "the application" of the skills and techniques he shares.

Stu works internationally to help companies involved in long-term relationship selling achieve greater results. In particular, Stu focuses on the insurance and financial services industries and is a member and Gold Resource Partner of GAMA. He is a member of the Richardson Chamber Board of Directors and a past member of the board for Prevent Blindness Texas. Stu is also President for Leadership Richardson Alumni Association and President for the National Speakers Association of North Texas for the 2011-2012 year. In the past he has taught business classes at Dallas Christian College and developed an online sales management course at the University of Texas, Dallas.

**Stu Schlackman**
Email: stu@competitive-excellence.com
Website: www.competitive-excellence.com

Follow Stu:
www.facebook.com/stu.schlackman
Twitter: @Schlackman

# Falling Forward

### By Carla Spurgeon

***Dedicated to William and Carolyn Ashley for always encouraging me
to think bigger and beyond!***

"Mr. Ashley, I have some good news and bad news for you today. The good news is that your daughter is coming out of the semi-conscious state she has been in for the past 3 days. The bad news is that she is hanging from the traction bar by her leg."

Can you imagine being greeted by the hospital nurse this way?

So why was my father at the hospital visiting his almost 3-year-old child? It's quite a story!

First, let me take you back to Detroit, Michigan in October of 1964. My family had just moved to Detroit from Traverse City. Dad was working as a cook and attending Wayne State. Mom was taking care of my younger brother Mitch, born in January, and my almost three-year-old self.

We had only been in the 3rd story apartment between 2nd and 3rd Street near Woodward Avenue for a few days. Detroit was not the safest or quietest place to be; however, it was still a few years before the famous riots of 1967. The Beatles had performed two concerts in September in the 15,000-capacity Detroit Olympian. Lassie would be the Grand Marshall for the J.L. Hudson Thanksgiving Day Parade that year.

As Mom recalls, it had been a normal day. There were 4 of us and our cat, Tibby. We had gone for a walk earlier in the day and were now back in the apartment. It was Sunday. Mom was ironing and Dad was at work.

Mitch was in his crib; I was running around the apartment as only a busy energetic child could! One minute I was in the room with her and the next thing I knew, I was pressed up against the screen to see where the voices in the alley were coming from. The screen was loose and with my inquisitive face pushed up against it, there was no stopping either of us – screen or Carla.

There was a Baptist minister and his wife living on the 1$^{st}$ floor of our building. The wife was standing in her kitchen when she saw me go flying past the window on my way down. We learned later that the Baptist minister had held a special service that night to pray for me.

Being a Sunday afternoon, there were several people nearby who saw me fall. Some were helpful, some not so much. It was like any other alley in the city, full of broken asphalt, concrete, gravel, and dirt. Not one cushy bush or grassy area to land on.

As Mom realized what had just happened and was racing down to the street for me, my baby brother Mitch was left alone in the apartment. A woman from across the street offered to help. She ran up to our apartment, grabbing Mitch and some baby food, and left a note for my mother so she would know where to come get him later. Thank goodness for a few nice neighbors!

Meanwhile, someone tried to flag down a female driver to help us, only to have her refuse and drive off. To this day, I don't know why, but maybe she was just afraid to get involved. A medical student happened to be walking through the alley at that exact moment and he flagged down a driver who stopped to help.

I was swooped up off of the ground and into Mom's arms for the ride to the hospital. Time was of the essence so we did not wait for an ambulance. Since the driver worked at Receiving Hospital of Detroit, he knew the fastest route and drove us there. Even though it was not the closest hospital, his ability to get us there quickly was worth the time saved.

When the fire department finally arrived, they were upset about the broken screen. Loose screens are still a common issue with children – the screen is simply not strong enough to stay in place when it is pushed against.

The parents are the first to be questioned in accidents involving children, so there were questions and accusations aimed at Mom. Did she push me out the window? Was she angry with me? Was I climbing on the window sill putting myself at risk? How did I manage to push the screen out?

Each year, more than 5,000 kids are injured by falling out of windows. That's an average of 14 children per day. Of these, the majority are toddlers under the age of five. According to an article in the Journal of Pediatrics, less than 1 % of these result in death. For those who land in a bush or on the grass, the injuries are often very minor, just scrapes and bruising. For those of us that do not have the luxury of a cushioned landing, injuries can be much more severe.

The younger children seem to fare better than the older ones because they don't always understand what is happening to them so they are relaxed while free falling. Common times for accidental falls are between noon and early evening which is generally play time for the under 5-year-old age group.

Over the years, I have heard many stories of that fateful day. My Dad, who was working at the time, was rushed to the hospital in his kitchen whites. He was mistaken for a staff member and sent into the emergency room instead of being left in the waiting room.

The fact is that I fell three stories into an alleyway in Detroit. Think concrete and asphalt, dirt, stones, concrete bits and gravel. Not a place where you would want to fall off a bicycle or even stumble, yet I fell three stories. (One story is generally thought of as being 10-12 feet.)

I was in a semi–conscious state for the next three days. My right leg was broken and a painful IV had to be inserted into my left ankle as I was too small for the IV to be put into my arm. My right cheek had a sharp piece of stone embedded in it. The extent of damage to my facial nerves on my right side is still unknown. The extent of damage to my brain would be unknown for years.

Thankfully, I have NO memory of the fall, the hospital or any of the trauma I endured. And thankfully again, this happened before it was automatically assumed that my mother might have caused my fall out of the window so she was spared that line of questioning by authorities. Had it happened today, any number of child protection agencies would have gotten involved, removed my brother from our home, and eventually allowed our family to be restored after a stressful investigation of Bill and Carolyn's ability to provide a safe home for their children.

The good news is that I *did* survive and have had only minor difficulties over the years because of the injuries sustained that day. The scar tissue in my inner ear from the impact of the fall has caused me to have a hearing loss that is part of my daily life. Early on, we discovered that I was a gifted lip reader – gifted as it comes naturally to me without any training. That's the acceptable side of the injury.

The down side was that I had vertigo issues throughout puberty because of scar tissue in my inner ear between the tiny little bones. Talk about growing pains! Riding my bike or walking down stairs became major events, not simple activities, as I could easily black out or get dizzy and fall. And I did. More than once. Living in the country, I'm not sure whether it was a blessing or a curse. There are fewer ways to get hurt, but enough to make parents and grandparents worry.

My family tells about my father taking me to see the Thanksgiving Day parade with the cast still on my leg and how excited I was to see the parade. I don't recall seeing Lassie as the Grand Marshall, though I'm sure I did. As the story goes, he had me on his shoulders so that I could see well. I could see alright! I was giggling and kicking him with my cast! Helpful strangers offered to hold me for a few minutes at a time so that he could take a break. While I was a small 3- year-old, the cast was bulky and heavy, especially when repeatedly kicked against a man's shoulder!

The cast itself was one of those things that you had to experience to know how bad it was. As my skin was drying out from the lack of moisture or being bathed, it itched. To counter the itch, I would stick pencils and crayons into whatever cracks (at the top of the cast) I could create so that I could scratch myself. Mom kept telling me not to do that; however, I persisted. I had managed to kick the heel portion of the cast into dust over the course of time. When I insisted on having a bath, Mom set me up with a plastic bag over the whole cast area, put me on my little school chair and gave me a shower.

When the doctor went to take the cast off, I remember being warned that it would tickle and I was going to need to be very very still or I could be hurt by the saw. It tickled and I wasn't hurt so I must have restrained myself that day. To my mother's relief, they did not find any broken pencils or crayons when the cast was opened up. However, I am told the cast stunk to high heaven!

One of the concerns expressed to my parents was my ability to walk normally after a fall of this nature. Physical therapy was recommended and I was ultimately able to take tap and ballet dance lessons. Those dance lessons and treating me as normal as possible served to help me have a fairly normal childhood. I was never allowed to think I was any different from the others. A few years later, we moved back to the small town my mother grew up in and close to her parents. I lived in that small town from age six to age seventeen.

There was nothing really remarkable about growing up except the tests we had done when I was sixteen to find out the extent of the damage to my hearing and possibly any brain damage that might have been caused in the fall. So many medical advancements had been made and there was talk of having surgery to restore my hearing loss. But the corrective surgery had only a 50/50 success rate back in the 70s so the decision was made to wait until I was of legal age and could decide for myself if I wanted to take that risk. The 50 percent in question was an uncertainty as to whether I would have any hearing left after surgery.

As for brain damage, there was none. Years later I would be able to laugh when the chiropractor hinted that she could see areas where adjustments should be done since my head "wasn't on straight." If she had only known how close she was to the truth!

Did any of this stop me from enjoying life? Never! Mom says it slowed me down only a little ... very little. Instead, it served to help me see that I had been blessed to survive and thrive. The bumps in the road became just that ... bumps, not obstacles. I learned to take detours when things were not going the way they should, and to have a good attitude about those hardships.

There is a bible passage that I am reminded of on a regular basis.

*No temptation has overtaken you except what is common to mankind. And God is faithful; he will not let you be tempted beyond what you can bear. But when you are tempted, he will also provide a way out so that you can endure it.* (1 Corinthians 10:13 NIV)

The Greek word for tempted also means tested. When I think about the life I've been blessed with, I see this as the case.

There were many times when I could have taken a different path, blamed God for my loss of hearing, the scar on my face from being cut by the stone I landed on, and for the number of times when I was redirected into activities that might not put my back at stress just in case there would be an injury and upset the delicate balance of what we knew was safe. I didn't participate in any sports in school. I wasn't drawn to team sports, and liked to push myself to the next level more than beat some other team.

Knowing that I was blessed to be alive and that God had my life in His hands, I felt it was only natural for me to want to "give back" in some kind of mission service. As a young adult, I joined a Christian Theatre ministry and traveled the USA extensively, performing for churches, schools, and military bases. My first day on the job set the pace for the next 10 years with that company. When I arrived at Los Angeles Airport, fresh from the small farm town I grew up in, I found that my transportation situation had changed and I was soon on the Flyway bus to Van Nuys. I think I must have looked a little lost when I got off the plane with my little blue suitcase in one hand and my purse in the other. Instead of running home, I jumped into the changes with both feet and grew more confident in my ability to adapt.

Cell phones and the Internet were not available at the time which made regular communication with friends and family a challenge. Having already established a fairly independent spirit, it was a good fit for me to live without my family for months at a time. Sure, I missed them; however, I learned that I could manage without seeing them more than once or twice a year.

Pretty soon I was traveling cross country in a van with people I didn't know and sometimes didn't like much at first. We would perform in different cities, in different situations and for different audiences. We ate foods I had never heard of and stayed in homes I would never have chosen to go to with people that we had to learn to trust would take care of us. It was an adventure of a different kind.

Sometimes the adventures in life are amazing to behold. Once when we were returning to our home office in Los Angeles, we were driving through the southwest at night. Without realizing it, the driver had passed the last gas station for about 100 miles or so. Back in those days, there were signs that told you that this was the last gas station for 100 miles or something to that effect. We found ourselves in a van that was running very low on gasoline. Someone in the back started praying and it wasn't very long before the driver noticed that the gas gauge had moved back up to where it appeared that we now had enough gasoline to make it to the next station. We actually got just that far. Had I not believed before that, it would have certainly given me cause to believe in miracles that day!

Oftentimes the message was simply to trust God. As with the gasoline, there were other adventures with automobiles over the years. One time we were in Oklahoma during a bad snow storm. After driving for hours in the snow or ice, we heard a loud crack and what we thought was a blowout. In fact, it was our driver side rear wheel being sheared off! This could have been a tragic accident for sure. The driver got us off the highway just outside Miami, OK. Again, we didn't have cell phones. We were able to flag down some help and connect to AAA for a tow truck to come get us off the road and into the local truck stop where we were able to be safe, warm and sheltered for the night. The next day we were able to find a local station to fix the van for us and were back on the road in good time. How can you doubt the presence of God when you repeatedly experience things like this?

Many times in life we fall. We have the choice to pick ourselves up, to be thankful that we are alive and well with minor injuries or to be angry at God or whomever was responsible for our "fall". I fell out a window and yet here I am, safe and sound.

Was it God's fault the screen in our apartment wasn't strong enough to withstand a 3-year-old? Was it God's fault that we missed our "last gasoline for 100 miles" sign? Was it God's fault that the wheel on the van came off in the ice? Let's turn those questions around a bit.

Was it God's guidance that put a medical student and experienced driver in the alley, as well as a minister in our apartment building to rescue me? Could it be that God's hand was at work taking care of his people when our gas gauge recovered as if the tank was being filled while we were driving? Was it God's hand that even in the small town of Miami, OK, we were blessed with AAA tow service and the right hands and parts to fix our van?

It was about 10 years later when I settled down and started working the 9-5 jobs. Having skipped the "college then career path," I was suddenly thrust into a management role with a convenience store chain with no formal training for the job, just a willingness to accept the adventure! When I moved to Dallas a few years later, that role continued with another company. Years of thinking on my feet served me well. However, it was not enough!

Eager to learn new skills and experience new adventures, I moved into a new career role – temporary staffing. I became "the temporary!" If I got bored, I knew there was a new assignment ahead. If I didn't know a task, I learned on the job. When I started as a temporary, I had no idea what fax machines or computers were about. One day they said, "Oh, we want you to take this assignment and you will need to know this particular set of computer skills." While I had the same place to go home to at night, each day was a different job and enough excitement to keep my sense of adventure alive.

One of the adventures that I have known and still love is my business as a direct seller. Driven to find a way to keep my acne prone skin in good shape, I found a direct sales company that met my needs and offered me a safe place to learn and grow in the business. It also gave me another benefit by providing me with leadership training and travel to other cities a couple of times a year.

During the day I was a temporary employee and a couple of times a year I packed my bags and flew to cities I would never have been able to visit otherwise. It was the best of all opportunities! Not content to play it safe, I learned how to book my own airline reservations, hotel reservations, rental cars and more. Pretty soon I was going out early and staying an extra day to enjoy the sightseeing. Friends would remark how they didn't know how I could get a rental car and drive a city like the locals without being nervous.

ADVENTURE!

On one of these adventures, I was able to take one of my sisters and enjoy a Bahamas cruise. We had a wonderful day on the beach enjoying the sunshine and embarking on another adventure. We signed up for the parasailing excursion. Remember how high I told you a "story" is? Well, now imagine that we were going to be flying over the ocean tied to a boat by a rope like a giant kite ride! And by choice no less! Fear of heights was not one of the things I learned from falling out that window! It was such a thrill to enjoy this wild ride! And true to my adventurous history and now adventurous spirit, we got our taste of the high seas that weekend when the ship had to reroute itself around what was to become Hurricane Katrina.

Since then, I have gone to Puerto Rico and taken a zip line excursion through the rain forest. While I was not alone, I didn't have the companionship of friends to buffer me from my moments of fear. Yes, I have MOMENTS where my common sense has to give my adventuresome spirit a good talking to about the wisdom of flying through the rainforest tethered to a strong wire! But on that day I didn't listen to that inner voice. I was drenched from the sudden afternoon rain forest shower that came down due to the upcoming arrival of a Hurricane and muddy from climbing a steep mountain path, but I was safe in my harness and hard hat.

Am I a daredevil? Hardly! I enjoy knowing where my base is. Routine is very important to me as it gives me time to regroup, regenerate and recharge before embarking on the next adventure. God didn't provide me with the tools to deal with life so that I could sit quietly in a corner and watch the world go by! He gave me a strong spirit that could enjoy and appreciate the adventures and thrills that life has for me!

How many times have you found yourself in a situation that has or could change the path of your life as you know it? Did you embrace the "fall," as a matter of record, or resent the change it represents? When you see the various ups and downs that I have experienced, does it give you a moment of reflection on your own experiences, both the positive and negative? What will you do the next time your face is pressed up against the screen and it gives way?

If you feel you're not living life to its fullest, I hope my story gives you the confidence to join me on the zip line. Life is an adventure.

LET'S LIVE IT!

Carla Spurgeon has led a full and vibrant life as a child of God, wife, and mother to several household pets. For the past 30 years, she has been a consultant and lineage leader with a direct sales party plan company. A charter member of the Direct Selling Women's Alliance, Carla has completed their Elite Leadership course and is certified as a Direct Sales Lifestyle Coach. Her website: YourLifeIsAnAdventure.com captures some of her best tips and ideas for creating your own adventuresome life!

**Carla Spurgeon**
Email: caspurgeon@hotmail.com
Website: www.myjafra.com/cspurgeon

Follow Carla:
www.facebook.com/carlaspurgeon
Twitter: @CarlaSpurgeon

CPSIA information can be obtained at www.ICGtesting.com
Printed in the USA
BVOW010124170113

310878BV00008B/58/P